The
Dalmatian

An Owner's Guide To

A HAPPY HEALTHY PET

Howell Book House

Howell Book House
A Simon & Schuster Macmillan Company
1633 Broadway
New York, NY 10019

MACMILLAN is a registered trademark of Macmillan, Inc.

Library of Congress Cataloging-in-Publication Data
Strand, Patti.
The dalmatian: an owner's guide to a happy, healthy pet/Patti and Rod Strand.
p. cm.
Includes bibliographical references.

ISBN: 0-87605-384-3

1. Dalmatian dog. I. Strand, Rod. II. Title
SF429.D3S88 1995
636.7'2—dc20   95–21234
                        CIP

Manufactured in the United States of America
10 9 8 7 6 5 4 3 2 1

Series Director: Dominique De Vito
Series Assistant Director: Felice Primeau
Book Design: Michele Laseau
Cover Design: Iris Jeromnimon
Illustration: Jeff Yesh
Photography:
  Cover photos by Pets by Paulette
  Courtesy of the American Kennel Club: 20, 21, 23
  Joan Balzarini: 96
  Mary Bloom: 59, 96, 136, 145
  Paulette Braun/Pets by Paulette: 2–3, 5, 11, 15, 16, 17, 22, 38, 44, 96
  Buckinghamhill American Cocker Spaniels: 148
  Callea Photo: 19, 30, 32, 45, 51, 53, 57, 58, 62, 63, 64, 79
  Sian Cox: 134
  Dr. Ian Dunbar: 98, 101, 103, 111, 116–117, 122, 123, 127
  Dan Lyons: 27, 36–37, 62, 96
  Cathy Merrithew: 129
  Liz Palika: 133
  Janice Raines: 132
  Susan Rezy: 96–97
  Patti & Rod Strand: 24, 31, 43, 48, 72, 73
  Judith Strom: 8, 29, 96, 107, 110, 128, 130, 135, 137, 139, 140, 144, 149, 150
  Jean Wentworth: 40, 47, 75
  Kerrin Winter & Dale Churchill: 7
Production Team: Troy Barnes, John Carroll, Jama Carter,
  Kathleen Caulfield, Trudy Coler, Victor Peterson, Terri Sheehan,
  Marvin Van Tiem, Amy DeAngelis and Kathy Iwasaki

Contents

Welcome
to the
World
of the

part one

Dalmatian

External Features of the Dalmatian

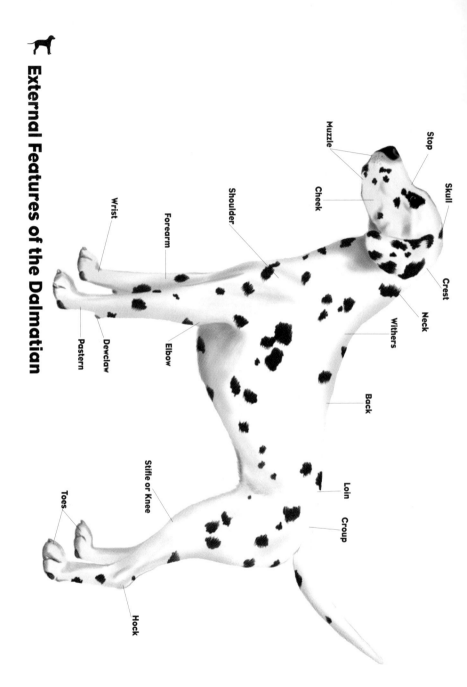

Skull
Stop
Muzzle
Cheek
Crest
Neck
Withers
Shoulder
Wrist
Forearm
Elbow
Dewclaw
Pastern
Back
Loin
Croup
Stifle or Knee
Toes
Hock

chapter 1

What
is a
Dalmatian?

Curious about what a Dalmatian is? Go ahead, ask a hundred Dalmatian owners "What is a Dalmatian?" You'll get a hundred different answers. Some of the responses may have similar themes, but they unerringly lead to the conclusion that Dalmatians are, in a word, unique. The reasons people choose them?

> "Their ability to keep up with outdoor activities." (jogging, exercising or going on camping trips)
> "They're intelligent."
> "I use them for hunting."
> "They're gentle with children."
> "I compete with them." (in conformation, or obedience or agility trials)

"Because they sit on your feet while you peel potatoes in the kitchen."

"Because they work well with horses."

"They're smart, alert protectors."

"They really do smile."

"They keep you on your toes."

"Because they demand pats and affection and always give it back."

"They seem to be able to choose my friends better than I can."

The list goes on and on and on. Dalmatians are magicians, successfully adapting to a wide range of owners' lifestyles—from high-energy activities to porch rocking. Their uniqueness, as observed by each owner, stems from their attentiveness to, and preference for, human companionship. Despite their athleticism and ability to be on the go all day long, they'd really like nothing better than to be with their owners. They don't like hunting more than they like their owners. They don't like retrieving more than they like their owners. They don't like chasing rabbits or digging for moles or playing with other dogs more than they like their owners. They are decidedly "people dogs."

WHAT IS A BREED STANDARD?

A breed standard—a detailed description of an individual breed—is meant to portray the *ideal* specimen of that breed. This includes ideal structure, temperament, gait, type—all aspects of the dog. Because the standard describes an ideal specimen, it isn't based on any particular dog. It is a concept against which judges compare actual dogs and breeders strive to produce dogs. At a dog show, the dog that wins is the one that comes closest, in the judge's opinion, to the standard for its breed. Breed standards are written by the breed parent clubs, the national organizations formed to oversee the well-being of the breed. They are voted on and approved by the members of the parent clubs.

The Same, but Different

Aside from the unique relationships they develop with their owners, though, they're all the same, right? Well, not exactly. Granted, they are dogs with black or liver (dark brown) spots on white coats; are medium-sized, weighing about 45-65 pounds and measuring 19 to 24 inches in height at the withers. But to leave it at that is like saying that all cars are the same because they have four wheels and an engine. If you look closer, individual Dalmatians vary in looks as much as individual humans do. For instance, if you go to Russia or France or Australia, Dalmatians will look surprisingly different in each of those countries, and they will vary in looks from those found in the United States. And within the United States, Dalmatians have distinctly different features, too.

One way Dalmatians keep looking like Dalmatians is through the use of the American Kennel Club registry system and adherence by breeders to a written "breed standard." This standard is maintained—and adjusted from time to time—by Dalmatian breeders who are members of an AKC-recognized "parent club" for the breed. This form of association (the AKC as a registry that also recognizes one national club which protects and promotes the interests of each specific breed) enables breeders of all dogs to compare their breeding efforts to a written description of a "perfect example" of what a dog of the breed should look like, how it should act and what it should be able to do.

Every Dalmatian is a unique individual—from his spots to his character.

This all sounds fairly straightforward and uncomplicated, but the complexity of genetics makes breeding "the perfect dog" about as easy as making an exact replica of a bowl of spaghetti, down to the precise placement of each knotted noodle, meatball and fleck of parmesan cheese—blindfolded. Actually, it could be argued that the spaghetti replication would be easier because you would be working from a physical model. A breed standard is *written*. Consider how frequently everyday conversations are misunderstood because of the many different meanings words can have and you will realize why the standard has nearly as many different interpretations as there are breeders in the country.

7

In fact, you can see this diversity for yourself. If you go to the annual Dalmatian national specialty show and look closely, you can see marked differences in weight, size, shape, symmetry, expression, movement, body tone, coat condition, eye color, dentition and, yes, spots. You will most certainly see 400 to 700 exquisite Dalmatians at a national because competition is fierce—but you will also find vast individual differences. And within these differences lies one of the keys to the popularity of dog shows. Each variation you see among the animal entrants represents a different interpretation—a different idea if you will—of the breed standard and what a Dalmatian should be. *Almost every breeder/exhibitor at the show thinks his or her Dalmatian is a better than average representation of the breed standard (and maybe even really the best one there!).* It's also a certainty that each breeder and exhibitor at the show feels that his or her Dal is the most unique and lovable one at the show.

Alertness is part of the Dalmatian's general appearance.

Studying the Standard

For someone who has not owned or bred a Dalmatian, the best way to get to know them is to read the standard while thinking of a dog that was bred to be a running escort for carriages and the people riding in them. Then go look at live examples at dog shows or wherever you can find them, and ask questions endlessly (you can do this if you confess that you're a wide-eyed novice—and you can get some interesting answers for comparison). In this book, you'll see why the Dalmatian has a notable affinity for horses and people. In terms of athleticism, you'll also discover that the Dal is more like a gymnast than a weighlifter or a football linebacker or a basketball or baseball player (even though he does scratch himself occasionally).

With this in mind, let's look at the standard. The **general appearance** emphasis on distinctive appearance, poise, alertness, lack of shyness and an intelligent expression relates directly to the Dal's human orientation and coach-dog duties. The Dal was selected with an emphasis on service and eye-catching appearance.

He had to have the self-confidence to be among people, vehicles, horses and the clatter of the streets without losing composure or attention to its duty, which was to protect the horses and clear the path for safe and swift passage of the carriage. The beer wagon pictures you may see with the horses charging and the spotted "Bowser" sitting next to the driver aren't exactly what the original breeders had in mind. No, the Dal was bred to work tirelessly at the side, front, back or underneath the carriage, clearing the road. He had to have enough intelligence to make decisions on his own about what did or did not constitute an obstacle to the carriage's progress, and he had to have the ability to do whatever it took to get rid of the obstacles. He had to do this while running inches from flying horses' hooves and iron-rimmed wheels which could flatten him in an instant. It's easier to see why the standard demands a specific temperament—one a fighter pilot would admire—and a high level of intelligence (and yes, you can see intelligence in the Dal's expression). An easily distracted, shy, or dumb dog would not last long doing a Dal's work.

Looks and Action

The Dalmatian's distinctive markings have also been preserved by careful breeding programs throughout history. The spotted coat not only sets Dals apart from all other breeds, but if you think of the rough-and-tumble aspects of his fire wagon escort work, it's obvious that his tasks were easier when "road obstacles" saw him coming and knew what he had in mind. For horse drawn carriages that transported ladies and gentlemen, the Dal's work was less frantic, but still necessary, and the markings were a stylish plus (just try to picture another breed acting as a carriage escort—it's almost impossible).

Well, if he's so darn smart and good looking, why *doesn't* he ride alongside the carriage driver? The simple and honest answer is that a Dalmatian does what he does because he loves to do it. It's in his blood. Only after he's done his work and after the carriage has stopped, will you find him nestled on top of the rig next to the driver. What about today with no carriages to speak of and cars that go too fast for Dal escorts? Well, joggers know that Dalmatians will run farther than other breeds of dogs, and will still keep that "intelligent expression" and "Can I go again?" look even though their tongues may be hanging three feet long. They've even been known to cut or scratch themselves somewhere along the way, but show the injury only after the run was over. Fatigue, age, cars, squirrels, people and bird distractions—none of it matters. *It's in the blood,* and it's there from the start. (With regard to fatigue and age, Chapter 7 will deal in part with how much strenuous exercise is appropriate for different age levels.) Younger Dals will run themselves silly—even to their detriment—if their masters are not careful to monitor their activities and force them to stop and rest at proper intervals.

The **general appearance** also asks for a dog that is not exaggerated or coarse and is symmetrical in outline. These aspects do not really speak for themselves until you are able to compare several Dals at once. Qualities like being overweight or underweight, in or out of good coat, or exaggeration or coarsness are best gauged against competition. The standard reflects that coarseness does not lend itself to the nimbleness and quickness found in a Dal or the required distance running. The symmetrical outline contributes to ease of movement in endurance situations. Combined with the size requirements, these standards produce a dog that has one of the highest agility-to-strength ratios in the entire dog world.

The exaggeration mentioned in the standard could relate to any aspect of the dog. You may find an exaggerated bend of stifle or a body that is too long or too short (or too "cobby," meaning chunky, and too compact). The dog may have too much or be too thick in bone (think of comparing yourself to a Neanderthal); too long a muzzle; a head that's too large in relation to the rest of the body; or the front half of the dog may look like it doesn't "match" or balance with the back half (for comparison, think of the exaggerated differences, front-to-rear, that are preferred in the bulldog). Aside from structure, the dog may have exaggerated spots (too big or too many)—but that's really covered under the color and markings portion of the standard.

Balance and Symmetry

The Dalmatian is a balanced-looking, symmetrical dog. It does not look like it was bred to subdue thieves or burrow in long tunnels for vermin. It was bred to run effortlessly, with endurance and a fair amount of speed—not the fastest dog of all, but the fastest long-distance runner. The symmetry assists in this process: if you asked for a "square" appearance, you would not get the effortless, endurance of movement that is characteristic of the Dalmatian. If you asked for a body that was distinctly longer than it was tall (with height measured at the withers, and length from point of shoulder to tip of rump) then you would get a topline that would be less fit for endurance runs. The standard is trying to say that it is better to be a touch longer than tall, but the overall balance of the dog is most important.

Notice the variation in spots in this pair of Dalmatians.

This balance and symmetry is important, because the standard also qualifies height. Under **size, proportion and substance,** it is desirable to have a Dalmatian that is 19 to 23 inches at the withers. Dogs under or over these dimensions are faulted for being too short or too tall. Measurements are taken with a wicket. A wicket is a U-shaped metal device which, when turned upside-down and placed on the ground, allows only 24 inches of space beneath the bar. It is placed on the dog's withers while the dog is standing in a normal posture. If they are over 24 inches at the withers, they're disqualified from competition. The reason for the size requirements is that once they rise above 24 inches at the withers, it's almost impossible for them to gait with the desired Dalmatian movement. We have seen *one* dog in twenty-five years that was over 24 inches at the withers and that still moved like a Dalmatian. One dog only. A Dalmatian with proper size and proportion will run the socks off another that's over 24 inches at the withers.

When you read the standard's **head** section, it looks almost like an artful dodge. *What is* fair length and free of loose skin? What's an alert, intelligent expression and what is this "balance" thing again? Maybe one of the best ways to think about balance and expression is to remember that Walt Disney's artists spent literally hundreds of hours with many Dalmatians before they started drawing them for the animated classic, *101 Dalmatians.*

They got it right—especially the **expression**—but only after long and careful observation. A note on **expression:** the AKC Dalmatian breed standard was revised in 1989 to its present form. The previous standard called for eyes to be "set moderately well apart, and of medium size, *round, bright, and sparkling, with an intelligent expression . . .*" The

THE AMERICAN KENNEL CLUB

Familiarly referred to as "the AKC," the American Kennel Club is a nonprofit organization devoted to the advancement of pure-bred dogs. The AKC maintains a registry of recognized breeds and adopts and enforces rules for dog events including shows, obedience trials, field trials, hunting tests, lure coursing, herding, earthdog trials, agility and the Canine Good Citizen program. It is a club of clubs, established in 1884 and composed, today, of over 500 autonomous dog clubs throughout the United States. Each club is represented by a delegate; the delegates make up the legislative body of the AKC, voting on rules and electing directors. The American Kennel Club maintains the Stud Book, the record of every dog ever registered with the AKC, and publishes a variety of materials on purebred dogs, including a monthly magazine, books and numerous educational pamphlets. For more information, contact the AKC at the address listed in Chapter 13, "Resources," and look for the names of their publications in Chapter 12, "Recommended Reading."

deleted portion (italicized) was a hotly contested element in the breed standard revision within the Dalmatian Club of America. A substantial number of breeders had very strong feelings about the sparkle in the eye that contributed toward an intelligent expression. In our view, some dogs will look you in the eye as a matter of course (not in aggression) and some will not. When a Dalmatian looks at you with the "sparkle" noted in the previous standard, you get the feeling that you're looking at a friendly, intelligent and potentially mischievous being, one with sense enough to roust the household at the scent of smoke and at the same time with humor enough to "put a pie in your face" if you get too serious. We named our kennel Merry Go Round for a number of considered reasons, one of which was the importance of having an alert and intelligent expression, which can be noted especially in the eyes.

We've talked a bit about balance already. The Dalmatian is a paragon of balance and moderation. You don't want a big head on a little dog or vice-versa. Similarly, you don't want an extremely elegant head on a male dog or a very "doggy" (remember the coarseness comments) head on a bitch. Again, this has to do with size and balance, and to some extent with sex. The females are generally more feminine versions of the males and this male/female difference should be apparent. The head should have clean lines and the Dalmatian should have a clean (not drooling or loose-lipped) mouth. The standard does a good job of describing **eyes, ears, stop, muzzle, nose, lips** and **scissors bite;** and it also notes appropriate size and angle relationships.

With regard to **eyes,** the major faults of ectropion and entropion eyelids refer to lids that turn *into* (entropion) or *out from* (ectropion) the eye. Trichiasis is a condition of one or more misdirected eyelashes, causing corneal or conjunctival irritation. These conditions are extremely rare to find in the show ring, but the fact that they have been carried forward in our breed standard (which was originally modeled after the British standard) indicates that these conditions have caused trouble in the past and are serious enough to be used as screening factors when making current breeding program selections.

After reading the standard's section on the **head,** the important thing to keep in mind is that the more you deviate from what the standard describes, the more you move away from symmetry, balance and intelligent expression. For contrast, picture a Dalmatian with close-set, yellow eyes, no stop between the forehead and top of muzzle, and uneven planes between the top of the skull and its pointy-nosed muzzle when viewed from the *side.* If, for instance, a line drawn across the top of the skull was parallel to the ground and another line drawn across the top of the muzzle pointed more toward the ground, the dog would be "down-faced" and less intelligent looking than one with parallel planes. Such a dog does not have the intelligent expression desired in a Dalmatian. Not even perfect spotting could save the conformation standard short-comings of a head like this—with these features it would look more like a varmint than a Disney dog.

The **neck, topline, body** segment calls for a smooth (no excess skin folds) throat and a nicely arched, fairly long neck. the word "arched" denotes a curved structure: a Dal's **neck** is not a stovepipe. The topline should be smooth, without a dip or break between the withers and the back.

The **chest, back, loin** and **croup** descriptions are clear, with reference to the illustrations. **Tail** docking refers to removing any portion of the tail, whether it's done at birth or later for any reason, through surgery.

In the **forequarters** and **hindquarters** segments, the front legs are to come straight down from the elbows to the pasterns, whether looking at the dog from the side or the front. **Cowhocks** occur when the points of the hocks are closer together than the heels of the pads in normal standing position.

The **feet, coat** and **color and markings** sections are reasonably clear. Most people, until they've seen a **patch,** wonder what one is. If you've ever seen a pointer with a black patch over an eye or covering an ear and a portion of its skull, that kind of marking is similar to a Dal patch. A patch is larger than a normal Dal spot, and is present at birth. When they occur, they are usually found on the head, but they can occasionally be located elsewhere on the body or tail.

The Dal's markings may be understood a bit better if you realize that genetically the dog is a solid black or liver-colored animal that also carries a gene for covering over the black or liver color. Genetically speaking, for any breed of dog that carries variations of this "white masking of the black or liver base color," the pattern of dark markings can show up in looks ranging from torn splotches of dark color to perfectly round dots of varying sizes. Selective breeding will determine how the dark markings appear. Theoretically, if you consciously selected *away* from the white masking (that is, you bred for larger and larger dark markings), you could wind up breeding a solid black

Genetically, the Dal is a black or liver-colored dog with a gene for covering the black or liver.

or liver-colored dog. But then it wouldn't be a Dalmatian anymore under the standard's specification.

This explanation of white masking over the dark base color also helps explain the standard's concern with **tricolor** markings. The tan point markings on a black and tan coat combination—as in Coonhounds and Doberman Pinschers, for example—are on the head, under the neck, and on the chest, legs and tail. The Dalmatian base color is supposed to be *pure* black or liver—without tan points. If you had a black and tan base color pattern masked by a white coat, you could see the tan points of that pattern *only* if the white masking happened to allow the dark base color pattern to show through on parts of the head, neck, chest, legs or

tail. That is where you would see the tan points showing through, and that is in fact where the Dal standard
looks for the tan tricolor markings. They are, as the
standard indicates, rare in the breed.

The Dal's **gait** is peculiar to the breed (and indeed,
peculiar within the breed—not all of them are built
perfectly enough to do it). The standards of efficiency,
endurance and power call for a movement that
is "steady and effortless." To use another word, considering the Dal's role as an escort, you could call the gait
"businesslike." When
the Dal is working
in his gait—especially
alone off leash—its
head position is for-
ward (not erect), held
slightly above the top-
line (at about 9:30 or
10:00 if a clockface ref-
erence is used). His
gait at an endurance-
paced trot is a smooth,
powerful version of a

*There are many
aspects of the
dog a judge
must consider
before picking a
winner.*

military double-time marching cadence. It has the
extended reach and drive noted in the standard, which
are combined in an effortless power, rhythm and
smoothness that is distinctive to the Dalmatian. This
has to be seen to be recognized—no amount of verbal
description will provide true awareness of what it really is. Seeing it is difficult, because it is hard to find:
although many Dals may get close to the desired gait,
fewer than one in a hundred will achieve it to perfec-
tion.

For **temperament,** refer to our earlier discussion of the
Dal's original purpose. This standard requires a stable,
highly intelligent, decisive yet polite Dalmatian to
properly represent the breed. The Dal's temperament
is another one of his distinguishing features, which will
be detailed more fully in Chapter 3.

chapter 2

The Dalmatian's Ancestry

Chasing down the Dalmatian's ancient history is fascinating, and reminiscent of being at a dog show years ago when a Harlequin Great Dane escaped from its handler and raced around the show site and neighboring area for hours while people frantically tried to recapture it. The Dane became, in the space of three hours by word-of-mouth descriptions, a Harlequin Great Dane, a Dalmatian and a Pointer. The descriptions also multiplied the Dane from one lost dog to three escaped kennel mates. Some people who described the escapee as a Dalmatian swore that they had seen it running through the show grounds.

Thus it is with the origin of the Dalmatian: Its history has been talked about, written about and guessed at for so long now that nobody *really* knows. But it's entertaining to note the number of serious people who swear they've seen it running through the show grounds of history. A spotted dog has been recorded as early as 3000 B.C. in a colored painting in the Tomb of Redmera at Thebes on the Nile. Subsequently, many other places of origin have been proposed, including Dalmatia (in southern Yugoslavia near, the Gulf of Venice in the Adriatic Sea), France, Italy, Spain and India. They have been referred to in various ways, too, for example: as a Hound, the Spotted Dog of Holland, as a Pointer, a Great Dane, a Common Harrier, a Bengal Harrier, a Large Bull Terrier, a Bengal Gundog, and an Istrian Pointer (which came from crossing mid-European pointers with small harlequin Great Danes). And they've been noted for work as guard dogs, gun dogs, hunters, coaching dogs, entertainers and even pickpockets.

One of the best research summaries on the Dalmatian's history is found in Alfred and Esmerelda Treen's book *The Dalmatian: Coach Dog—Firehouse Dog* (Howell Book House, 1980). Considering that the Dal's origin cannot possibly be pinpointed with existing data, the Treen's chronology of eighty historical comments becomes an intriguing study of the basic human urge to explain things with limited information.

The Dal Did It All

For instance, in some historical observations, the Dal is credited with being a hunting dog, preferring feathered to ground game. We have seen Dals hunt on their own, chasing both ground and feathered game and catching both. Some

---

WHERE DID DOGS COME FROM?

It can be argued that dogs were right there at man's side from the beginning of time. As soon as human beings began to document their existence, the dog was among their drawings and inscriptions. Dogs were not just friends, they served a purpose: There were dogs to hunt birds, pull sleds, herd sheep, burrow after rats—even sit in laps! What your dog was originally bred to do influences the way it behaves. The American Kennel Club recognizes over 140 breeds, and there are hundreds more distinct breeds around the world. To make sense of the breeds, they are grouped according to their size or function. The AKC has seven groups:

1) Sporting, 2) Working,
3) Herding, 4) Hounds,
5) Terriers, 6) Toys,
7) Nonsporting

Can you name a breed from each group? Here's some help: (1) Golden Retriever; (2) Doberman Pinscher; (3) Collie; (4) Beagle; (5) Scottish Terrier; (6) Maltese; and (7) Dalmatian. All modern domestic dogs (*Canis familiaris*) are related, however different they look, and are all descended from *Canis lupus*, the gray wolf.

accounts credit the Dal with being a natural coaching dog, but add that the instinct is not present in all members of the breed (some have no interest and cannot be taught to coach). Some swear that the dog has been reported as originating from Dalmatia; but some who had been to Dalmatia found that no one there could recall (or knew relatives or elders who could recall) spotted dogs either working in that area or as a dog native to that area. The remarkable thing about tracing references to the Dal's past is how little hard information exists in comparison to the enormous amount of speculation and logical deduction used to explain their origin.

The Dalmatian was bred to escort coaches.

All things considered, it is prudent to say that spotted dogs have been documented historically, and that spotted dogs have been versatile companions, field dogs and protectors. Regardless of the guesswork as to ancient sightings and specific skills, reports of dogs that clearly resemble what we would recognize as Dalmatians today exist from as early as the mid-seventeenth century. At that time, they were described as coach dogs. Descriptions of Dals as coach dogs in England became common as early as the 1800s. Hence, from the 1800s forward, his work and association with coaches, horses and people have created the niche he occupies in the contemporary public mind.

Naturals With Horses

Judging from their tendencies to work with horses, hunt for game, clear the barn of rats and mice, chase squirrels and birds and catch moles, it's pretty clear that the Dalmatian has parts of its family tree in both the Sporting and Terrier groups of dogs. Some Dals are more inclined to hunt (and catch) game than others; some are more willing to jump into the water

FAMOUS OWNERS OF DALMATIANS

George Washington

Pablo Picasso

Gloria Estafan

Melanie Griffith & Don Johnson

Richard Pryor

Paula Abdul

Eugene O'Neill

Richard Simmons

19

than others. Some chase cats, some nuzzle them. Nearly all of them are unafraid of horses and can be trained to work well with them, which the horses seem to understand.

It's always an amazing process to behold when you see behavior bearing out a genetic tendency to *do* something that's never been taught. From the first time you feel a nip on your Achilles tendon from an Australian Cattle Dog puppy (one that has had absolutely no coaching in this area at all), to the time you get to see your first field trial with dogs who have been trained to do what they do best, it always leaves one with a bit of wonder about what untapped talents are coursing within our own veins. It's also uplifting to see the absolute joy that each dog takes in applying its inherited skill.

Dalmatians have served as many things to many people, as this half-century-old photo shows.

Historically, the Dalmatian was probably used for hunting and guarding, and as a palace decoration. The reason it is found in the AKC Non-Sporting group is because it has been used to hunt, as a military dog, as a coach dog, a horse barn dog and as a family pet. It may not have the nose (or the need) to compete with the best hounds and it may not "live for retrieving" like a water dog, but the Dal can do both. It has successfully competed in field, obedience, agility and conformation trials. In addition, the Dal has been a stage performer, is still widely known as the fire station mascot because of its duty with horse-drawn fire wagons, has served in K9 military duty, and as a therapy dog for elderly people. This varied background has produced a dog that today can do nearly anything to the satisfaction of almost any owner.

Who would own a Dal? The owners are nearly as varied as the Dal's interests. Our first president, George Washington, and statesman and presidential candidate Adlai Stevenson both owned Dalmatians. Notable Dal owners also include artist Pablo Picasso; singer/recording stars Gloria Estefan; Paula Abdul and John Davidson; fitness guru Richard Simmons; psychic Peter Hurkos; ex-mayor of Los Angeles Sam Yorty; entertainment industry personalities Melanie Griffith and Don Johnson, Richard Pryor, and Darren McGavin; opera singer Ezio Pinza; New York jazz artist Bobby Short; Arthur Fiedler of Boston Pops fame; and, of course, playwright Eugene O'Neill, whose "Last Will and Testament of an Extremely Distinguished Dog" has become a classic.

The Dalmatian's past role was definitely a combination of utility and showpiece, considering his coach dog work and distinctive appearance. Perhaps because of the automobile, which put the coach dog out of a job, his popularity in the United States re-

mained fairly stable until most recently. The Dal was a relatively unique pet in American households until about thirty years ago. At that time, a combination of events fanned the flames of interest in Dalmatians.

A 1938 photo of (l-r) Ch. Princess Ha'Penny of What Ho, Ch. H.R.H. of What Ho and Ch. His Majesty of What Ho.

The Impact of *101 Dalmatians*

The Walt Disney production of *101 Dalmatians* was released in the 1960s and was an instant success. The public (including children) loved it. The Disney Studios loved it, too, because the animated characters and the story were timeless. In a perfectly planned business strategy, Disney pocketed the proceeds from the original release, put the movie away, and re-released it every seven years until the late 1980s, after which it was sold as a video. This release strategy coincided with waves of children reaching seven years of age and rekindled interest in Dalmatians every seven years. The effect of this was relatively continuous publicity for Dalmatians. Other movies began to use Dalmatians in them (*Tucker,* for instance). Then, in the 1980s, fashion, design and advertising discovered the splash Dalmatians added to pictures. When David Letterman filled his studio with forty-seven Dalmatians and let them ham it up in a live, chaotic, off-leash uncontrolled scramble (not a sedate, animated Disney story), the message was undeniably clear: Dalmatians were now stars.

From horse-drawn fire wagons to modern fire engines, the Dalmatian has remained the fireman's mascot.

Suddenly, Dals were no longer in the barn schmoozing with Nashua. There were relatively steady gains in registrations during the *101 Dalmatians* re-release years, but for the last ten years or so, Dal numbers have been climbing more rapidly. Recent annual AKC figures have shown Dals among the ten most popular breeds in the country. In 1995, they ranked ninth among AKC breeds registered. Considering their rise in popularity, the people in the country who really deserve a gold star are the breeders. Despite the increase in registrations and heightened public interest, breeders have done phenomenal work in improving Dal temperament, health and conformation over the past twenty-five years. It's a phenomenal achievement because increases in popularity and numbers can signal the beginning of the end of quality in a breed. It hasn't happened to Dalmatians, and with proper care and responsible ownership and breeding programs, it doesn't have to.

A nineteenth-century rendering of the "Black Spotted Dalmatian Berolina."

What happens when the general public becomes enchanted with a breed is that enthusiasm leads some people to dream about "becoming breeders." Some go to dog shows, read books, talk to breeders and conclude that they would enjoy owning a family pet more than breeding. Others jump in without a clue and discover three to five years down the road that what they're doing isn't working, and that animal husbandry is *far more* than a casual preoccupation. It is a commitment to a demanding lifestyle in which achieving even modest goals is difficult and could take five to ten years or more. Both sets of people may start out with good intentions, but uninformed breeding and mistakes by inexperienced breeders can leave genetic messes that actually reintroduce or reinforce problems that serious breeders fight like crazy to avoid or eliminate. The stabilizing of Dal registrations rates most recently could be an encouraging sign that more people are taking responsible, informed approaches to owning versus breeding Dalmatians.

chapter 3

The **World**

According to the
Dalmatian

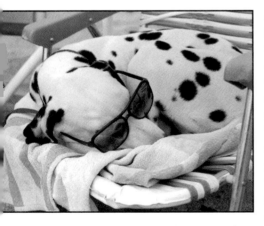

Although Dalmatians love to ride in the car to just about anywhere, they're not back-seat dogs in any other sense of the word. (They're also not the kind of dog that has to be in your lap or face while you drive, either.) Their inner world contains wonders around every corner and no dangers that are quicker, tougher or smarter than they are. A Dalmatian is not a "porch dog" that sits and looks at a guest or visitor until some unknown cue prompts it to get up and investigate or greet. They are instantly curious about nearly everything and won't hesitate to go see what's up.

The Dalmatian breed standard calls for poise and alertness generally, and a stable and outgoing—yet *dignified*—temperament. You should understand that this translates into a dog that does *not* go wagging up to any stranger and lick them up one side and down the other. This means that when a Dalmatian meets strangers, he usually prefers *to go up to them at his own pace,* investigating fairly thoroughly before becoming the wagging, silly bouncing friend. Many people are so taken with the dog's looks and bright expression that they forget introductions and manners. They'll rush up to the dog, arms and hands extended, bending down, with body language that says to the Dal, "I want to grab you and pet you and touch you." The Dal *understands* the body language to say "I want to grab you and hold you in one place and prevent you from moving around me and checking me out while I check you out."

Bred to Judge Safety

Remember, the Dalmatian was bred to take control of the streets and make judgements on whether things were safe or not for the horses and masters. You can't make judgements while you're being held in one spot and examined. This isn't to say that the Dal's instincts should dictate your routines, or that he can't be trained to be appropriately sociable; however, they are more likely to meet someone by going through the steps of investigation and judgement before acting like a wagging fool.

What if they *don't* like someone after investigation? Sometimes this happens, and most of the time it's for reasons the owners can't comprehend. When this occurs, it's rarely an aggressive scene. The Dal's reaction is more likely to be one of avoidance, perhaps a quiet grumble or groaning and a move to the next room, from which he can keep an eye on things until the stranger leaves. Your first impression as an owner is to feel like scolding your dog for unsociable behavior. But after breeding dogs for twenty-five years and seeing a dog remain anxious around a person on about five separate occasions, we'd have to say that the Dal's judgement has always turned out to have an element of soundness. We have no idea what they're looking at or smelling, but they have an innate sense of safety and concern for their masters. This instinct, even if not readily explicable, is definitely part of the genetic foundation for Dals.

As an example of this kind of concern, we placed Jack, an adult male, with a friend whom we had known for a few years. This friend had always wanted a dog, but his wife didn't. His wife's reluctance was also the reason he wanted an adult rather than a puppy, which would need housetraining. The wife continued to dislike the dog, citing house dirt, dog smells and another dish to wash. But the husband loved jogging with the dog, and their two small children loved him, too. So Jack became a member of the family by majority vote, even though he was an uninvited guest as far as the wife was concerned.

One winter evening after she got supper started, the wife opened the back door to let the dog in. Jack wasn't there. She looked around for signs of dirt or dog in the house and could find neither. She couldn't find her two-and-a-half-year-old daughter, either. Alarmed, she looked outside the house and next door. No one had seen her. It was 5:30 p.m. and dark outside. The wife searched the immediate vicinity and called her husband and the police. The husband came home and the whole neighborhood joined in the hunt, but the toddler couldn't be found. The dog, by this time, had slipped everyone's minds.

A DOG'S SENSES

Sight: With their eyes located farther apart than ours, dogs can detect movement at a greater distance than we can, but they can't see as well up close. They can also see better in less light, but can't distinguish many colors.

Sound: Dogs can hear about four times better than we can, and they can hear high-pitched sounds especially well. Their ancestors, the wolves, howled to let other wolves know where they were; our dogs do the same, but they have a wider range of vocalizations, including barks, whimpers, moans and whines.

Smell: A dog's nose is his greatest sensory organ. His sense of smell is so great he can follow a trail that's weeks old, detect odors diluted to one-millionth the concentration we'd need to notice them, even sniff out a person under water!

Taste: Dogs have fewer taste buds than we do, so they're likelier to try anything—and usually do, which is why it's especially important for their owners to monitor their food intake. Dogs are omnivores, which means they eat meat as well as vegetable matter like grasses and weeds.

Touch: Dogs are social animals and love to be petted, groomed and played with.

Finally, at around 7:30 p.m. the police called the household and asked whether they owned a Dalmatian. They said yes, and that he was missing, too. The police responded, "Well, ma'am, we think we've found your daughter. We're a couple of miles away from your house, but she's with a Dalmatian and we can't get close enough to her to pick her up. Could you come and get her?" Jack had a completely loving—and tolerant—home after that. Jack is gone now, but the family yard still has a Dalmatian in it.

The above incident was even more poignant because Jack had never had any training in protection or what to do in case of danger. He had only been trained to go to an occasional dog show (he did win his AKC championship)

Most of all, Dals love to be with their owners.

and run around the yard and house. Period. Experience with Dals will sooner or later lead you to the conclusion that those with good breeding and a loving home will have an innate sense of what to do in terms of safety, watchfulness and keeping the peace. Training could professionalize this sense (Dals have been used as K9 Corps military dogs), but it doesn't seem necessary for the ordinary household.

Mischievous and Smart

Before you get the impression that the Dal's world is all business, duty and doing the right thing, there's something you should know. They're sometimes mischievous and a bit too big for their own britches. As for intelligence, we once raised a Dalmatian and a Golden Retriever who were born within days of one another. The Golden was destined for a Canine Companions for Independence program (in which dogs are extensively trained to help people who are disabled). We had to train the Golden for basic obedience commands during the first year of her life with us. After that, she was destined for "college" and on to even more complex training. We noticed during her training sessions that the Dal puppy—without intention on our part—was watching and learning the basic commands, too. So, we started including him in the sessions.

One result of this pairing was a startling comparison of learning rates. The Dal would learn the commands in half the time that it took the Golden to "get it." On the other hand, once the Golden got it, she did it every time. The Dalmatian? Yes, he understood quickly, but once he got it, the next time you gave the command, he'd hear it, remember it, look at you, and then decide whether he really wanted to do it or not. Sometimes he would, but often he would not.

Suddenly, a number of things became crystal clear. For one, it's a little more obvious to us now why Dalmatians are not the largest entry in most obedience trials. For another, we had long ago noticed that Dals would figure out how to do something that you *didn't* want them to do around the house, and when you let them know it was not allowed, they would think of another method to achieve the same end. Once they were told that the second method was not allowed, they'd think up a third, and a fourth, and a fifth, developing as many as ten different ways of doing the forbidden thing. Other dogs, like the Golden, would get the hint after one or two episodes, and give up the undesirable behavior.

It is this tendency to invent new ways to do naughty things and the capacity to remember and figure out new methods that can drive Dal owners nuts. It can become a contest of wills, which has its hazards: if the Dal gets the idea that persistence and ingenuity will produce a reward (if he "wins" the contest) you have created a relationship where he thinks there are no limits to what he can get if he just applies

CHARACTERISTICS OF THE DALMATIAN

Curious about everything

Alert

Innate concern for master/family

People-oriented

Mischievous

Quick learners

Exuberant greeters

himself. The owners, on the other hand, may decide that their dog is incredibly knotheaded and does not learn. Actually, the dog *has* learned—or at least has the mistaken impression that he is smarter than his owner, and that he should be able, with enough effort, to get his way in any area he desires.

If at First Your Dal Does Succeed . . .

A Dalmatian owner has to be smarter than his or her dog and must be consistent with regard to rules of behavior. This consistency is also required of everyone else in the household, because if the Dal discovers that one person in a three- or four-member household allows him to do a certain thing—say, jump up—and the other household members do not, he will generalize this discovery to the entire human population. Hence, he will try jumping up on guests, visitors and strangers on the street, thinking that one out of three or at least *some* people will allow him to jump up. The Dalmatian's natural persistence, tenacity and inventiveness could make him a nuisance in the hands of a lazy or unresponsive owner. Like small children, Dals *will* get your attention, one way or another.

Dals are quick learners, but invent new ways to do what they want.

But once they get your attention, they don't always know what to do with it. Sometimes they give the silliest looking apologetic grin imaginable. One of the curious characteristics of the Dalmatian is the ability to "smile." To some people it looks more like an ear-to-ear silent snarl than a look of glee, and to others it appears to be an embarrassed grin. In any case, when some Dalmatians get flustered, they draw up their lips and pull back the edges of their mouths, exposing almost every tooth in the same movement that you or I would use to smile—but they're not laughing.

29

Smiling Dogs

They *look* like the fox who just cleaned out the hen-house with no one the wiser, but the smile usually only appears just after they've been discovered in the kitchen with the contents of an entire garbage sack carefully spread all over the floor, or when their master uses a scolding tone of voice, or when they've just found and shredded another roll of bathroom tissue. It's actually a look of supplication ("Don't throw me out of the house! I couldn't help myself, honest!") and it's apparently a genetic recessive trait. The smiler will lower his head and often slink while displaying the look. Although it appears most frequently when Dals know they've done something that will get them into hot water, it also shows up in isolated cases. We had one Dal that would smile only when someone would take out a cigarette.

A curious characteristic of the Dal is her ability to smile!

The reason it's hard to tell whether they're smiling is that they are bright enough to be suspicious characters whenever anything goes awry. In some cases they almost certainly must "think out" the situation in order for them to occur the way they do. For instance, one of the things they love to do in an open area is play their form of dodge ball. In their version, they use their bodies as the ball. They will run away to about twenty-five to thirty yards and come rushing back straight at either another dog or you, running at full tilt for a direct hit, and missing by a fraction of an inch. Their goal is to get as frighteningly close to you as possible without hitting you. Your role (or the other dog that's playing) is to stand completely still, without flinching. The winner whizzes by without crashing into you; you're a winner, too, if you stood like a statue. Who is the loser in the game? Well, sometimes, if you see them coming and make the cowardly move of trying to get out of the way (choosing to dodge the wrong direction), you'll wind up being grazed or flattened by a fifty to sixty-five pound projectile. When this happens, and the master screams in outrage, a smiler will smile.

We actively discourage this game, so the dogs don't play it much with us. But if they get an open field and the chance to run, they invariably play the game with each other.

We've seen them play this game in a field where one dog would run around in circles as wide as 150 yards in diameter before whizzing by his target. On at least one occasion, the "whizzer" ran around until the "whizzee" got bored with the game and started sniffing more interesting things on the ground in the field. On the next turn around the circle, the whizzee had his nose in the middle of an attractive smell on the ground and was standing completely still, but the whizzer chose to smack him with a direct hit on the way by. The whizzee was knocked headfirst into the object of his investigation, soiling himself from the jaws down to his paw. The whizzer *had* to be laughing.

Dalmatians love the water.

These examples are not intended to reflect badly on Dals—or Golden Retrievers. The important thing to remember is that the Dalmatian's amazing capacity for physical activity and endurance seem to be matched by amazing bursts of genius as well. They will test your patience and keep you on your toes, but they are also as devoted as they are smart.

Attention Sets Boundaries

The key to having a good relationship with a Dalmatian—whether it becomes a member of the family as an older dog or comes as a puppy from a litter—is in the amount of attention and affection with which you establish boundaries of behavior. They are eagerly responsive to attention, games, praise and positive strokes. They have a memory like an elephant, however, for coercive, negative or harshly corrective actions. They will respond much more readily to rewards for approximating desired behavior than being forced into the position or pose or posture you wish them to assume.

The difference, for instance, in holding out a reward until they sit versus pushing down on their hindquarters while pulling up on their lead while commanding

them to "sit!" lies in two critical areas. They will more readily and consistently respond to a "sit" command taught through play learning, and they won't start calculating how they can avoid you or avoid sitting, or get back at you for the "pushy" approach to training. No dog is happily responsive to abusive training prac-

Dalmatian puppies displaying typical exuberance.

tices, but the Dalmatian has a peculiarly sharp memory for affronts. They generalize here, too: if they have had a bad experience learning how to sit, they're almost certain to resist other obedience lessons which take on the same manipulative tone.

With regard to the Dal's energy level, the impression exists in some quarters that buyers must beware that Dalmatians have nervous temperaments, excessive energy and are hyper. This sweeping generalization is unfair to the breed, because good temperament has been a specific focus of breeders for the last twenty years, and much wonderful work has been done in this area. There is little question that in any planned breeding program, you *can* select for bad temperament just as you can select for good temperament. Parentage, pedigrees and the variety of genetic possibilities force breeders to contend with that possibility: It's one of the conscious considerations in every breeding decision. Consistent choices toward good temperament will move the whole breed toward freedom from shyness but also, possibly hyperactivity, as Dal breeders have demonstrated over the last twenty years. But notwithstanding such care, the possibility still exists that on rare occasions, the gene pool may produce a dog ill-equipped for coping with the world.

When a person unacquainted with Dals approaches a Dal home and is greeted by a full-grown adult dog, sometimes impressions can be misleading. There's no question that Dalmatians get excited when someone— even a familiar friend—comes on the property or to the door. They sound the alarm and want to be the first one there to check out the visitor. Proper training will take care of any barking or control problems in this area, but guests who are greeted in this manner, especially people who have heard that Dals are "hyper," could easily confirm what they have heard by the excitement they first see. Hopefully, they will stay long enough to see the exuberant greeting followed by the normal pattern, which usually includes happy acceptance followed by settling back down for a snooze under the dining-room table or in front of the fireplace. But, they shouldn't be too surprised to see that when they're ready to leave, the Dal wakes up and treats their departure with similar gusto.

If puppies have been raised in a calm environment with their mothers; if they have been touched, petted and handled regularly by the breeder; if they have been properly vaccinated and wormed; if they have been weaned to a good quality puppy chow; if they were taken from their litter by their new owner no earlier than seven weeks of age; and if they were introduced to their new home life with kindness, thoughtfulness and sensitivity then chances are good that you won't see any behavior abnormalities.

Understanding Shyness

If you see behavior that you fear to be shyness within a litter, note that puppies in a whelping box regularly run over one another and try to see if their brothers' and sisters' ears will chew off from five to eight weeks of age. They also establish a pecking order during this period of time. The pecking order demands recognition of who's the biggest and most dominant male or female and who's next and so on. The ones on the bottom of the pecking order are the quieter ones, who cover their ears and get run over the most. They may go about their business at some distance away from the other puppies, and they may squeal and squirm to get back to their box when you pick them up, but that doesn't necessarily indicate shyness. Shyness is more like having a puppy regard you as a horrible monster even after you've gently picked it up and cuddled it two or three times. (And even this reaction can be related to other causes. For example, as puppies open their eyes, their first reaction to actual visual recognition of your face as you hold them and look at them is often one of startled horror—even though you may have picked them up and calmly snuggled them without incident numerous times before their first real live glimpse.)

The low puppy on the totem pole will not give you an indication of how he will act in your home. We once picked a beautiful puppy that was rather subdued in the litter—at least third or fourth down in the pecking order. Once he got away from the litter, he grew into a multiple Best in Show winner with one of the best show dog attitudes anyone had ever seen (and he had one of the best housedog temperaments anyone could possibly desire). In the vast majority of cases, there is a good temperament inside each puppy. It will bloom in response with the love, nurturing and careful discipline provided by the new owner. Chapter 4 elaborates somewhat on how to do this.

MORE INFORMATION ON DALMATIANS

NATIONAL BREED CLUB

Dalmatian Club of America, Inc.
Mrs. Anne T. Fleming, Corresponding Secretary
4390 Chickasaw Road
Memphis, TN 38117

The club can send you information on all aspects of the breed, including the names and addresses of breed clubs in your area, as well as obedience clubs. Inquire about membership.

BOOKS

Ditto, Tanya B. *Dalmatians*. Hauppauge, N.Y.: Barron's Educational Series, 1991.

Gregory, Geraldine. *Pet Owner's Guide to the Dalmatian*. New York: Howell Book House, 1994.

Nicholas, Anna Katherine. *The Dalmatian*. Neptune, N.J.: TFH Publications, 1986.

Treen, Alfred and Esmeralda. *The New Dalmatian, Coach Dog—Firehouse Dog*. New York: Howell Book House, 1992.

MAGAZINES

The Dalmatian Quarterly, Hoflin Publishing Inc., 4401 Zephyr Street, Wheat Ridge, CO 80033-3299.

VIDEOS

American Kennel Club. *Dalmatians*.

Living
with a

part two

Dalmatian

4

Bringing your
Dalmatian
Home

Bringing your Dalmatian home is actually a part of a process that should, whenever possible, start with an introduction to your puppy from the age of three or four weeks. Whenever *possible* should be emphasized, because some breeders will not allow outsiders to handle or look at their puppies until they've had their first shots. If, however, you have located a breeder who has a litter that happens to have a puppy that you think you might like, try to get acquainted with the puppy as early as possible. The puppy will remember your scent when it comes time to take her into your family, and she'll adjust to your home easier.

Learning About Puppies
One of the things to remember about puppies is that they don't do much else than eat and sleep and crawl around looking for another

38

meal for about the first three weeks. The mother provides most of the stimulation in their lives. From about three weeks to five weeks of age, they begin to notice each other, but they still function mainly in the eat and sleep modes, and play little. From the age of five weeks, they start their pecking order and dogdom social education by playing with one another, picking on one another, learning how to get along in a group and learning how to let the others know when they've had enough. It's at this age that the puppies look a lot like the Disney Dalmatians, rolling and frolicking after one another like a barrel of monkeys.

There are a few points to remember about this sequence of litter growth. First of all, if you get a chance to see a three- to five-week-old litter of puppies, and they do nothing but awaken from a drowse and walk around sleepily for two or three minutes and then pile up and go back to sleep again, it's not necessarily a sign of sloth or low I.Q. They are simply eating, sleeping and growing at this stage. Secondly, because they are actively forming a pecking order and pack social order, size plays an important part in the outward appearance of individual personality when the litter is together. The puppy that's two ounces heavier may rule the pack and overshadow the others, and the remaining individuals in the litter may be holding back some of their own personality in deference to the leader.

As noted in the last chapter, one of our Best in Show dogs was an obviously beautiful puppy who stepped aside every time the litter leader—who was himself a very pretty puppy—ran through the room. The puppy we picked didn't blossom with his own personality until he came home with us, but then he became one of the most eager, friendly, tail-wagging show dogs we ever had.

One of the lessons for the novice looking for a pet is that a breeding line with good personality characteristics tends to reproduce those personality traits. So if you don't see it in the litter box (as in the case of the

PUPPY ESSENTIALS

Your new puppy will need:

food bowl

water bowl

collar

leash

I. D. tag

bed

crate

toys

grooming supplies

puppies overshadowed by the "alpha" or "pack leader" litter puppy), it doesn't necessarily mean that an actual absence of zeal exists. The thing to watch for is a defensive puppy who exhibits frightened behavior whenever stimulated by either other puppies or people. This caution does not include the puppy that simply stays beyond the reach of your hand or runs away from a larger puppy; rather it's the one who is consistently alarmed by and frightened of outside stimulation. You'll rarely find this trait if the breeding line is producing good temperament.

Learning From the Litter

One other consideration is that for the first seven weeks of puppies' lives, they are learning how to form relationships with each other. They're *also* learning their approach to relationships with other dogs in general. The litter box relationships that naturally blossom amongst terriers are markedly different than those of St. Bernards, Chihuahas or Dalmatians, but the point

Puppies are curious creatures, but need rest, too.

is that each puppy—regardless of breed—*must* undertake this learning at these ages; otherwise, they may be confused about how to interact with other dogs later in their lives. The puppy that is taken from the litter before seven weeks of age may fear other dogs as an adult. Because this learning stage exists, leave them with their litter for a minimum of seven weeks. If you don't, you may wind up with a dog that bonds wonderfully with humans, but—especially as an adult—displays unacceptable behavior (usually based on fear) in reaction to other dogs.

One final thought on litters through seven weeks of age: it is almost impossible to set a price on puppies before seven weeks of age. This is especially true for Dalmatians, because things like nose and eye pigment may be uncertain through eight weeks of age or more; structural considerations may also be impossible to evaluate before they're ready to be ranked for relative quality in the litter, and the prices will most likely vary according to qualitative distinctions. So if you go to see a litter and fall in love with a particular dog, don't be surprised if the litter owner has a difficult time setting a price on the puppy before seven or eight weeks of age. They're not trying to see how much money they can pry out of you; it's more likely that they're unsure of the final relative quality level of the puppy within the litter.

The breeder should be able to give you a price range, however, and this may help you in your deliberations. Regarding prices, you might keep in mind that any number of dog publication articles have entertained us by figuring the "profit" on litters, based on time spent on labor, veterinarian and medical attention, stud services, advertising and so forth.

Contrary to the popular misconception of those outside the field and newcomers to dog breeding, even if everything goes right in producing a litter, the hourly payback amounts to somewhere around $1.47 per hour for the litter owner's time. It is truly a labor of love for the long-term breeder, and that's one of the reasons why the career span of the dog fancier usually lasts up to about five years maximum or is a lifetime commitment. Those people who stay "in dogs" for more than five years generally do so for the rest of their lives. Those who don't probably realize that the "dog game" has animal husbandry as its foundation (rather than profit, power, riches and fame) and get out of it before five years elapse. It's expensive when a litter winds up costing a breeder $2,000 in veterinary bills on top of a previously paid stud service, and most people who enter into dog breeding have no idea that their "tuition" might run so high, nor understand the level of responsibility required and the emotional and financial stress.

Time for a New Home

It's seven weeks, you've found a breeder who is willing to refer you to others who own dogs they've produced, or you've asked around and found them on your own.

You've learned that the breeding program produces healthy, good-tempered dogs, and the breeder let you look at the litter at four to five weeks of age. You saw a puppy you liked and found that she was in an acceptable price range, and you introduced yourself to her by letting her crawl into your sleeve, and around your neck, and nibble your ear; you let her do the same with each of your family members. The contract was signed, spay/neuter conditions agreed upon, and your fenced yard and house have been set up for a new four-footed family member. At last, it's time to go home!

You have to remember that this is a huge change for the puppy, from an environment of brothers and sisters and mom to a completely new set of sights, smells and sounds, including humans who are ten to twenty times or more larger than they are. Small wonder if they appear cautious or a bit frightened in reaction to their new setting.

HOUSEHOLD DANGERS

Curious puppies and inquisitive dogs get into trouble not because they are bad, but simply because they want to investigate the world around them. It's our job to protect our dogs from harmful substances, like the following:

IN THE HOUSE

cleaners, especially pine oil

perfumes, colognes, aftershaves

medications, vitamins

office and craft supplies

electric cords

chicken or turkey bones

chocolate

some house and garden plants, like ivy, oleander and poinsettia

IN THE GARAGE

antifreeze

garden supplies, like snail and slug bait, pesticides, fertilizers, mouse and rat poisons

Getting Used to a Leash

If you go some distance to pick a puppy up, remember to bring a leash with you. If your travel time exceeds the puppy's bladder or bowel limitations, you want to be sure to find a quiet spot where she can safely exercise on a lead. If this is the first time the puppy has had a leash on, *let her do all the leading* (if she moves toward an area that you do not prefer to visit, pick the puppy up and start over again—*do not pull her back with the lead*). Similarly, follow her quickly enough to keep the lead completely slack and *do not let the puppy "pull" you along* (if you unwittingly train her to pull on the lead, you'll regret it when you fly around the block after the puppy when she weighs 65 pounds).

The object with the lead for the first ten to twenty tries is to get the puppy used to wearing it and responding to *you* (to your voice direction, affection or reward) rather than to a tugging message from the collar and leash. This is your opportunity to have the puppy associate wonderful experiences with the leash. If done right, the dog will grow into one who jumps for joy every time you show the lead to her because she knows it means a walk or playtime or rewards and praise.

We have always used nylon choke collars and snap-ring leads of various lengths, depending on the activity. Flexi-leads, which fit in your hand and reel out and automatically wind back up, are one of the greatest inventions of the century. A Flexi-lead is too much for the puppy's trip home, but after she is happily accustomed to a walking lead (it'll take about a week or two at a minimum), you can use the Flexi to give more freedom during your walks. Be sure to remove the nylon choke collar whenever the puppy is free to move about on her own. A choke collar is great for control, but can be a hazard if left on the dog when she is unsupervised.

On the way home, the puppy could react with distress to the noise and vibration of the vehicle and of her departure from the litter. If so, she could show you the full strength of her vocal cords (they are usually about three times stronger than your eardrums). If the puppy is snuggled in someone's lap, the problem is usually solved. Another possible solution for anxiety is

Learning about obedience training early.

turning on the car heater. As it gets warmer, the puppy tends to want to curl up and sleep. As adults, Dals are wonderful travelers in vehicles, and some are also very good as puppies, but chances are, the first trip in a machine is likely to be a scary event.

What You'll Need at Home

When you get home, you should have, at a minimum, the leashes and collar mentioned above, a fenced yard, food, bowls for food and water and a sleeping quarters enclosure. Water must be available at all times up until 9 or 10 p.m., depending on when you go to bed. This restriction is the *only* exception to the water available at all times rule, and it lasts only until the dog is house-broken. (When we travel with adult dogs, they have a half-filled water container inside their crates during the trips. Even airlines will not accept dogs for shipment without cups for food and water attached to the shipping container.)

The water restriction from just before bedtime through the night for the puppy is to enable her to sleep as long as possible before she wakes you up to tell you she has to go outside. This will happen around six hours after bedtime for a week or so.

Your puppy should have something soft to lie down on.

Don't view it as an inconvenience, but as a wonderful opportunity to show the puppy that eliminating is done *outside* or wherever you have selected for exercise.

The puppy's sleeping quarters should have a blanket or soft cloth padding (have two or three pads dedicated to the puppy, so a clean one will always be available), and it should be small enough so that she will tell you when she has to go out to potty. The puppy will not soil her sleeping area. "Small enough" means, especially if the enclosure is a box or container, enough room to stand up fully with head erect, turn around and stretch, *but not much more.* If the container is too big, the puppy will simply bark at you once or twice, then go to one end of it and urinate or defecate if your response is too slow.

Housetraining Hints

If you use an airline carrier as a sleeping enclosure, you'll find that this container is one that the puppy soon will voluntarily choose to crawl into for a nap when she gets tired during the day. We use these as housetraining tools in the following way: for the first two to four weeks of adjusting to home life, we are with the puppy whenever she is loose in the house. If it looks like she has to void—if she starts sniffing around in small circles or looking around for an appro-

Your puppy needs a schedule to develop good habits.

priate spot to go—we pick the puppy up, take her outside, and stay with her until she urinates and/or defecates, and offer praise for success. We then bring her back into the house, still keeping her within sight. Whenever we have to leave the room momentarily, the puppy is enclosed in the crate until we return. When we leave the house, the puppy of course has access to the outside or an appropriate exercise area.

If you follow this routine religiously for two to four weeks, gradually providing supervised exposure to the rest of the house, it is possible to raise a dog that never has an "accident" inside the house. You are also cementing your relationship with the puppy by having her in the same room with you whenever you are together in the house, and you are also in a position to correct her behavior and set boundaries for activities within the house. For instance, if you notice the puppy becoming interested in the corner of the sofa or furniture legs, you can prevent her from ever committing her first chewing error.

45

Chew Toys for Your Pup

Chewing is normal for puppies—it's their hereditary way of communicating within the litter and is as natural as babbling is for human babies. You should have some chew toys for the puppy to use as intentional replacements when undesirable chewing tendencies are detected. If she goes for the TV knobs, give her a quarter-inch diameter composite chewing log. All Dals are incredibly efficient at destroying chew toys. The only one we've found that is apparently indestructible is the beehive-shaped rubber toy. These have lasted for years around both pups and adults, and they enjoy chewing them. An inexpensive thing that puppies will play with for days before they start to wear it out is a plastic pop bottle. If you keep the cap on, the container is too large to get a good grip on and the puppies will use it as a giant hockey puck whenever they see it.

Another caution with regard to chewing has to do with house, yard and garden plants. Identify the vegetation you have and call your veterinarian, your county extension service or a plant expert and find out whether your plants are toxic to dogs. They will chew on rocks, too, especially ones about as big as your thumb that are fun to toss around in their mouths. If you see them doing this, take the rock from them and dispose of it, telling them "No!" Some Dals will get carried away with sloshing them around in their mouths and before they know it, they swallow them. Having a pocketful of rocks surgically removed from your Dal's stomach is not the way you want to become acquainted with your veterinarian. There are also foods that are toxic to dogs, which are discussed in Chapter 7. Teaching a Dal what is and is not permissible to chew is generally a process that lasts the lifetime of the dog. They're constantly discovering new things to chew that you've never had to pass judgement on.

As a final note on chewing, it's cute to have the puppy untie your shoelaces or clamp surprisingly sharp puppy teeth on your fingers or wrists or forearm. It's *not* cute for a sixty-pound adult to do the same things. If you want a well-behaved adult, don't allow your puppy to continue its "chewing communication" with you. When she comes up and puts her mouth on anything that you wouldn't allow an adult to bite or chew, catch her in the act of starting to bite the object and snap her smartly on the end of the nose with your index finger, and tell her clearly (but without yelling) "No!" This kind of a correction will startle the puppy more than anything else, and you will find that she will direct her attention elsewhere almost immediately. Give the puppy praise when she changes her focus of activity to

something desirable. If you are consistent with this form of correction at an early age, you will wind up with a very well-mannered Dal.

It may look cute, but you have to nip chewing problems in the bud.

If you follow the simple guidelines discussed above, your trip home should be the beginning of a wonderful adventure and a devoted partnership that will last longer than a decade.

chapter 5

Feeding
your
Dalmatian

"What do you mean my dog is a little heavy?" The not-so-new owner returns with the puppy purchased nine months previously to show off, visit and to get more Dal information from the breeder. The breeder explains that the dog is carrying a little too much weight for good growth and health; that Dals will eat nearly everything that's put in front of them; and that balanced growth is important to structure, fitness, adult health and longevity.

It's *so* easy to let your Dalmatian get fat. It seems like an active dog—especially the marathon runner/gymnast of the dog world—wouldn't tend toward obesity, but with the variety of low-cost foods on the market that use animal fat for taste and filler elements to provide bulk, it's no wonder that our dogs can grow up looking like fast-food junkies.

One of the wonderful things about entering your dog in an AKC dog show is that you can get *instant* feedack on how fit your dog looks. If you have a Dal that is a few pounds overweight around the house, there's nothing to use as a model for comparison. They carry their weight fairly well, too. They don't develop rolls or bulges, they just get bigger everywhere. Sure, they may lose the graceful, tapered-in look in the neck and loin, and you may not be able to see the hips or the shoulder or the withers, but even if they're fat, they still have the strength and agility and energy that keeps them going long after you've collapsed from exhaustion. "*This* is a fat, unfit dog? This animal that runs me into the ground?" Take him to a show and find out. If your dog is five or six pounds heavy, it shows. If your Dal is even heavier than that, you don't feel like going out to share a hamburger after your loss. (Just as an aside, dogs never know they've "lost" at a show. They definitely know when they've won—they get as excited as you do. But their self-esteem never flags when they come home with a third- or fourth-place ribbon or even no ribbon at all.)

You don't have to have a fat dog. In fact, once you get past the Dal's tendency to test your intelligence to see whether *they* can control what you offer them and how much you feed them, it's fairly easy to maintain proper weight and muscle tone.

> ## TO SUPPLEMENT OR NOT TO SUPPLEMENT?
>
> If you're feeding your dog a diet that's correct for her developmental stage and she's alert, healthy-looking and neither over- nor under-weight, you don't need to add supplements. These include table scraps as well as vitamins and minerals. In fact, a growing puppy is in danger of developing musculoskeletal disorders by oversupplementation. If you have any concerns about the nutritional quality of the food you're feeding, discuss them with your veterinarian.

Eating Right From the Start

Let's start from the beginning. When the puppies are born, they live on mother's milk until weaning, which occurs gradually from three-and-a-half to five weeks, depending on the mother's instincts and breeders' practices. The puppies usually need to nurse no more than four-and-a-half to five weeks, but the mother will continue to play at nursing them, and will start to regurgitate food for them as they are in the process of weaning. Our experience with puppies is that they are willing to eat puppy chow that has been blended to a powder and mixed with warm water to a gruel consistency as early as three-and-a-half weeks. They start eating kibble puppy chow that has been soaked for at least fifteen minutes as early as four to five weeks. By the time they are six weeks old, they are usually well on their own, eating puppy chow kibble that has been soaked for ten to fifteen minutes in water.

We feed our puppies and pregnant and nursing bitches a premium growth formula kibble until they reach about one year of age (we switch the puppies to adult food anywhere from nine months to a year of age).

We'd like to mention that we've noticed over the past quarter century that it seems as if dog food companies are either constantly trying to improve their products, or are sometimes bought out by larger companies that have different ideas about quality and profit margin. In either case, formulas for dog foods are adjusted from time to time. The first indicator of such a change is usually your Dal's coat. It starts to blossom with reddish blemishes or rashes on the top of the head, along the spinal column and in the loin area. If you see an abrupt change in your dog's coat, compare the current ingredient list on your dog food container with an old label before you rush off to the dermatologist. It might hold a clue as to what's happening.

HOW MANY MEALS A DAY?

Individual dogs vary in how much they should eat to maintain a desired body weight—not too fat, but not too thin. Puppies need several meals a day, while older dogs may need only one. Determine how much food keeps your adult dog looking and feeling her best. Then decide how many meals you want to feed with that amount. Like us, most dogs love to eat, and offering two meals a day is more enjoyable for them. If you're worried about overfeeding, make sure you measure correctly and abstain from adding tidbits to the meals.

Whether you feed one or two meals, only leave your dog's food out for the amount of time it takes her to eat it—10 minutes, for example. Freefeeding (when food is available any time) and leisurely meals encourage picky eating. Don't worry if your dog doesn't finish all her dinner in the allotted time. She'll learn she should.

Mealtimes

Puppies need at least three meals a day through teething, which occurs at about four months of age. We usually continue the three meals per day routine up to five or six months, at which time we switch to two meals a day. Our adults remain on two meals per day. There is some research to show that single daily feedings and low body weight will result in longer lifetimes, but we have never been scientific enough to figure out how to feed once a day and keep the dogs in peak condition. In addition, when you feed the dogs once a day and have nothing else available, they have more of a tendency to clean out your garden or gobble up anything else edible on the property.

Your dog should have cool fresh water at all times.

Switching Foods

The puppies eat growth formula food for nine months to a year, as noted above. When the food gets too "hot" for them—that is, when they have grown to the developmental level at which the protein percentage in the puppy chow is too high for them (which will happen to every Dal), we switch to a kibble with 19 percent protein derived from low-purine food sources (the health chapter contains a more detailed discussion on food and nutritional risks for Dalmatians). Our dogs carry their weight well and have less shedding, more energy and brighter eyes, and they do so in a climate that is damp enough to grow almost any kind of opportunistic bacterial culture. Less shedding means exactly that: we have never found a nutritional or grooming cure for shedding. Dal hair naturally sheds, and each hair shaft has barbs which pull it into fabric like a small porcupine quill. Anyone who tells you that Dalmatians don't shed is fibbing. Anyone who tells you that they've discovered a food, food supplement, or shampoo or coat dressing that ends shedding is also having fun or trying to get rich at your expense.

Kibble Only

Both puppies and adults are fed dry kibble, period. We feed nothing else, because if you use a complete kibble that produces good weight, tone and health, you have fewer variables to consider when something goes wrong with your dog. For example, if you fed your dog table scraps, kibble, an occasional can of dog food as a treat or supplement, pet vitamins and dog snacks and treats, and your dog suddenly broke out in a rash, you'd have a more complex job of figuring out whether the rash was food-based. Straight kibble may sound boring, but if you do your research and buy the right kind, it will provide all the nutrition needed to produce a healthy, happy and long-lived animal.

Straight kibble also makes life simpler when you take trips. If you take your animals with you, packing up enough to last the trip is easy; or, if you know you can purchase it at your destination, you may not have to worry about carrying provisions at all. If you leave your dog in the care of a kennel or a trusted friend, instructions for feeding are almost foolproof.

When we feed both adults and puppies, we soak the dry kibble with water up to top of the kibble in the dish for ten to fifteen minutes before feeding. This prevents the food from hitting the stomach dry (as it would be if not soaked in water beforehand) and swelling inside the stomach; it also assists in

---

HOW TO READ THE DOG FOOD LABEL

With so many choices on the market, how can you be sure you are feeding the right food for your dog? The information is all there on the label—if you know what you're looking for.

Look for the nutritional claim right up top. Is the food "100% nutritionally complete"? If so, it's for nearly all life stages; "growth and maintenance," on the other hand, is for early development; puppy foods are marked as such, as are foods for senior dogs.

Ingredients are listed in descending order by weight. The first three or four ingredients will tell you the bulk of what the food contains. Look for the highest-quality ingredients, like meats and grains, to be among them.

The Guaranteed Analysis tells you what levels of protein, fat, fiber and moisture are in the food, in that order. While these numbers are meaningful, they won't tell you much about the quality of the food. Nutritional value is in the dry matter, not the moisture content.

In many ways, seeing is believing. If your dog has bright eyes, a shiny coat, a good appetite and a good energy level, chances are his diet's fine. Your dog's breeder and your veterinarian are good sources of advice if you're still confused.

water intake. The only drawback to soaking the food is that it does not stimulate the teeth and gums as the dog eats it, so having chew toys available and following sensible dental care practices become more important if you follow this method of feeding.

How Much?

How much to feed varies from dog to dog, and also varies depending on the dog's age. Youngsters will burn up more energy than old-timers, and smaller dogs will generally eat less than larger ones. You want your dog to look trim, (but not skinny) and athletic looking, with the last rib barely visible about the time the next feeding rolls around. Our adults eat anywhere from six to nine cups of kibble per day (the total of both feedings), depending on age, sex, time of year and individual level of activity. Once they get to middle age (around six to eight years) they tend to put on weight more easily than the youngsters, too. You will have to find the amount of food that produces the weight that looks best on your dog.

While searching for correct amounts of food, don't let your Dal snooker you into allowing poor eating habits.

Each dog should have his own bowl.

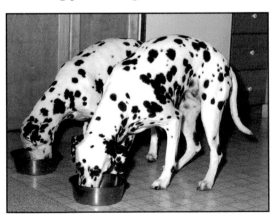

If the dog's successful with tactics such as finicky eating, starving until the treats show up, begging for table scraps and rooting out the garbage, these will be proofs that he can outsmart you. If we have a Dal that turns up his nose at a meal and is not showing any signs of lethargy, stress or illness, the meal goes to someone who will eat it. You don't have to do more than let one of the house-mates gobble down about two or three bites before the message gets across. The next time the dinner bell rings, a magical transformation usually occurs and the

53

reluctant eater returns to the dinner table as if nothing had happened at all.

No Appetite = Trouble

If *all* of our dogs turn up their noses at their food, we start examining the formula on the side of the dog food bag. Dals are notorious for their hearty appetites, and if they don't eat, start watching for whatever health sign they're giving you. You should be aware, though, that once a Dal is conditioned to table scraps or treats, it can go for an enormous length of time—sometimes two or three days—picking at or refusing common kibble, so sometimes it's hard to know whether a health problem or brattiness is the issue. Hence, another advantage to sticking with kibble for puppies and adults is that you will have far fewer problems in terms of attitude, health and behavior.

If this recommendation for basic kibble and a standard, fixed diet puts you in a quandary as to what to use as a reward for desired behavior, *think simple.* We have trained dogs to do everything from laying down and rolling over to "whispering" instead of "speaking" by using only praise and rolled up bits of whole wheat bread. They are more interested in you and what you are doing with them than they are in the kind of treat you are using to reward them. (It helps if they are trained just before mealtime, too.)

Because Dals are so relationship-oriented, it's easy to fall into the line of thinking that "they must be as bored as I would be if I had to eat the same thing they're eating." The next step in this thinking is to dream up things to feed them that would excite your own palate: maybe a piece of your pizza or the last bite of your burrito would be nice, and how about a sip or two of beer to slosh it down? And you *know* from the look on the dog's face at tableside how he would feel about a meatball from your spaghetti. And when your child sees you doing this, guess who gets the ear off the chocolate Easter bunny?

Don't do it! Keep it simple, keep it basic and keep your Dal healthy (see Chapter 7 for more details on nutrition). The meatball violates the purine guidelines, chocolate is toxic to all dogs, and you never really know what's inside a burrito. Follow the advice of an old handler friend of ours, a person who showed dogs for more than forty years and loved both the dogs and the wonderful opportunity to make a living working with animals. His words of wisdom were, "They're wonderful friends, and it's easy to start treating them like kids, but you always have to remember, *they're dogs,* and they'll do what dogs do." His comment applies in general, but in the case of food, dogs are especially notable for their tendency to eat—or at least chew—anything, some for no earthly reason. *Of course* they will respond with gusto to almost any food you eat, including all the spicy, sweet and fat-saturated snacks for humans—*they're dogs!*

Depending on You to Feed Them Right

What they really need, since they're domesticated creatures dependent on you for their health and longevity, is an owner who loves them enough to understand what the dog's body and activities are telling them. Keep an eye on firmness of muscle tone, look for minimal shedding, a blemish-free coat, brightness of eyes, a cool, wet nose and the normal energy level for your dog. You can get all of these qualities on a very basic feeding program with commercially prepared food, provided you know what you are looking for and properly match the food with the age and activity level of the dog.

chapter 6

Grooming
your
Dalmatian

Grooming your Dalmatian? What's to groom? They stay pretty much as they are, don't they? If you go to a dog show and look at the Poodles, Pomeranians and some of the wire-haired breeds, you quickly realize why handlers of the "grooming breeds" beg to show only in the afternoon (their entire morning is spent in final grooming preparations for their ring competition). On the other hand, a lot of dogs—Dalmatians, Italian Greyhounds, Viszlas, Rhodesian Ridgebacks—look like they need nothing more than a bath and toweling to be ready for the showring.

Because there's little coat to dress or otherwise style for a show, grooming is less trouble with a Dal than with many other breeds. But that doesn't mean there's nothing to it, and it also doesn't mean that

57

Dals who don't go to shows don't need grooming. They all need some basic care and they all love the extra attention that habitual grooming provides.

Coat

First of all you will notice, especially if you live in an area where it rains much, that all Dalmatians are mud magicians. They can get rain-soaked and covered with

mud, or collect grass stains and brambles, but if you give them a half hour in a clean, dry and padded sleeping area, they come out looking brand new. The only things that we've observed as permanent coat stains are real paint (when the four-footed helpers get too close to the two-footed painters) and black walnut husk stains (almost impossible to remove from anything, especially a white coat). Otherwise, they keep themselves clean nearly year round.

When you're getting ready for a show or a visit from Grandma, you'll probably want to put some

After trimming, you could use a grinder to smooth your Dal's nails.

finishing touches on your already stunning-looking pet. To do this, first shampoo with a pH-balanced shampoo in cool or tepid water. Some Dals take to water, some don't. You can bathe them in your shower, bathtub, an outside tub, or under an outside hose if it's warm enough. It's better in all cases if you have a nozzle that sprays a gentle shower and doesn't make a lot of noise. Wash the dog as you would your own hair: wet down, lather, rinse and repeat. Rinse thoroughly so you get all the soap out—then stand back for the dog to shake from nose to tail, after which you can dry him off with a thick cloth towel.

After the shower, do you notice discoloration or reddish stains in the wrinkles of the lip of the dog's lower jaw? Do you notice any reddishness in spots or bumps anywhere on the dog? How about the skin on the underside? Is it smooth, blemish-free and light pink or almost white? The red blemishes or shading in wrinkled areas are not a sign of dirt, but more likely an indication that the dog's diet might possibly need some adjustment. Dals, like other breeds and humans, can have allergies to specific things in their environment, but reddishness in the lower lip, on top of the head or elsewhere on the body should merit a consideration of food first. (See the chapter on health for information about this.)

If it is feasible, after using the towel, your dog should be able to run in the house or a clean area to air dry the rest of the moisture from its skin. After drying the dog completely, finish the grooming by clipping or grinding toenails, trimming whiskers and the loin area, and by thinning or trimming cowlicks and the tail as necessary.

Toenails

If you're lucky, you've had your Dal from puppyhood and have taught him to sit for toenail sessions and to expect a treat and oodles of praise when finished. If you're not lucky, you've *tentatively* cut his toenails or "squeezed" rather than "snipped" them, and have also committed the error of making sorrowful sounds of sympathy while doing the job. These things all teach dogs to be horrified of toenail care or even the anticipation of it. With enough of this kind of education, they can go into histrionics over toenail grooming, and you'll wind up finishing the job while they're hanging from the chandelier.

This well-groomed pair makes a pretty picture.

Whether on a puppy or an adult, toenails are a no-nonsense, no sympathy, matter-of-fact job, to be done

**GROOMING
TOOLS**

pin brush

slicker brush

flea comb

towel

matt rake

grooming
glove

scissors

nail clippers

tooth-
cleaning
equipment

shampoo

conditioner

with gentle but firm insistence, tons of praise and a treat at the end. Do the cutting or grinding quickly; trim *up to but not into*, the quick (the pink part inside the toenail), and reward effusively when you're done. If you have a puppy, do the trimming with a standard pair of fingernail clippers while you hold the pup in the crook of your arm or in your lap. If your Dal is an adult, you may want to do toenails while he is tethered on a grooming stand or standing on a bench. In either case, it's much easier to do if you take the trouble at an early age to make this grooming activity one which is "play" for the dog and which doesn't inspire fear.

The *reason* for doing nails, of course, is to prevent injury or infection from split or broken toenails. It's not just a showy excess. You don't have to go through more than one episode of an infected toe, or watch a veterinarian pull more than one painfully dangling toenail off, to know the blessing of healthy feet and the value of regular foot care.

Getting Used to the Grind

The tools for adult dog toenail care include grinders of the Dremel hobby type, equipped with a sandpaper drum, or mechanical clippers of the Resco type. If you use a grinder, expose the puppy as early as possible to the grinder itself first, and then to the noise of the grinder while you are using it for another task. It's the same process as getting a gun dog used to the sound of gunshots. Start with a low-volume noise that approximates the grinder and work your way up to full speed with the puppy in the room. You then work up to holding the puppy while you have the grinder in use (protect the puppy's eyes from any danger) and finally, to touching the dog with the running grinder and working your way toward exposing his feet to it.

If you are careful and persistent, and if you stay away from the quick while grinding, you should have a cooperative toenail patient forever. The three things that bother the dogs about the grinder the most are the whine of the motor, the vibration of the drum on the toenail, and being restrained for the job. With all three of these factors, the later the dog is introduced to toenail grinding, the greater the fear becomes.

Coat Trimming

With regard to cowlicks, the Dal typically has three areas that may require attention before entering the show ring. They are located at the front of the chest, the hip points of the buttocks, and from the bottom insertion point of the ear down the neck. All of these areas, when trimmed with a thinning scissors (teeth on one blade, cutting blade on the other), produce a smoother look which gives a subtle advantage in the show ring. The cowlicks at the breastbone run horizontally from the outside of the shoulders toward the center of the breastbone. To trim these areas, hold the scissors parallel to the cowlick ridge and thin it down to get rid of the ridge. The breastbone itself may have a cowlick, too. Thin it so the ridge disappears.

The same advice applies to the cowlicks on the rear. The object is to simply smooth down the hairline. The hair also tends to grow a little long and feathery along the backs of the legs from the hocks to about midway up the thighs. The thinning scissors can smooth this area, too. As for the tail, not all Dals have the same length of coat, so you may not need any more trimming than just to smooth the cowlick at the end of the tail. Sometimes, however, the tail may need thinning on the underside for about the last two-thirds of its length, which thinning scissors will take care of. If you trim the tail, make certain that when viewed from the side it tapers gracefully from the base of the tail to the very tip. It must be smooth, strong-looking and without a visual break from base to end.

Trimming the loin area cleans up the underline. There is a fold of skin that extends from the front of the thigh to the rib cage when the dog is standing in a show stack position. This skin fold is either shaped with an electric clipper or trimmed with a curved-blade, blunt-nosed scissors to make the line along the bottom of this skin fold clean. Don't misinterpret from this description of a clean line that the Dalmatian is supposed to have a "wasp waist," or a steep cut on the underside from the ribs to the tail. The Dal should have good strength of loin; weakness in this area would not enable long distance running or the strength, flexibility and agility desired in a Dalmatian. Again, the loin "look" reminds one more of a gymnast than a fashion model.

If the dog has redness between the toes or in the wrinkles of the mouth, a peroxide wash may help, and cornstarch has been used to lighten up the skin discoloration underlying the coat. The problem, though, may be one of nutrition rather than shampoo or coat conditioning.

With regard to whiskers, remember that they are found over the eyes; on the sides of the mouth and on each cheek; under the jaws in the center; and a little farther back at each side. Trim them off for a clean look. You may have read that if you trim your dog's whiskers, he'll either lose his balance or not be quite as smart

as dogs with whiskers, or otherwise act as if he doesn't have all of his marbles. You may also have heard that if you trim puppies', whiskers, they won't develop completely mentally. This is based on the fact that whiskers provide a sense of touch,

Your Dal looks to you to keep him clean and healthy.

which tells animals whether they can stick their heads or entire bodies down a varmint hole, or lets them know how close they are to objects in their environment (much like the little feeler spring wires that attach to the fenders of automobiles which alert drivers to curbs).

Trimming whiskers on our Dalmatians does nothing to make them clumsier or measurably dumber than other dogs. In fact, you could probably shave their entire bodies and still wind up with Dals that are smarter than about 90 percent of the other breeds. Smartness has never been a Dal problem (unless you happen to disagree with their conclusions—and that's really your problem, not theirs).

Regular curry combing will remove dead skin and hair.

Of course, a completely groomed dog also has clean teeth, ears and bright eyes. Care in these areas will be discussed in the next chapter.

Now that you have a Dal that is sparkling clean, properly trimmed and ready to make the rest of the dog world pale by comparison, the only thing left to complete the picture is the wagging tail, a distinguished and confident attitude and boundless energy to run and play until you are completely worn out. Part of the secret to the Dal's attitude is contained in the next chapter, on health.

chapter 7

Keeping your Dalmatian Healthy

About twenty-six years ago when we brought home our first Dalmatian, the breed did not enjoy the generally good reputation it has today—and with good reason. Dalmatians suffered a myriad of health problems and too often had unstable temperaments. If you asked a veterinarian about Dalmatians back then, you would often get a puzzled look and a cautious reply designed to find out whether you'd already made the mistake of getting one. Veterinarians were pretty unified in their distrust and dislike of Dalmatians, commonly advising clients against owning one. Luckily for us, our decision to get a Dalmatian was based on a childhood experience Patti had had with a wonderful Dalmatian named Pal who lived in her neighborhood. Her remembrance of Pal's sweet, playful nature over-whelmed all the criticism we heard about Dalmatians. Had we listened to the advice of the day, we might never have learned first-hand how wonderful life with Dalmatians can be.

Digesting Purines

In the late 1960s when we became Dalmatian enthusi-asts, veterinary science had long before (1916) discov-ered and documented the fact that Dalmatians possess a unique metabolism. Dalmatians handle purines, the parent substance for the uric acid compounds found in certain meat and vegetable proteins, more like humans and apes than like other dogs. Dalmatians will not thrive on diets high in purines, and some will develop serious, life-threatening health problems or die prematurely as a result of such diets. Dalmatians don't break down purines beyond the level of uric acid, whereas other breeds go a step further, convert-ing uric acid to allantoin before excretion. This trait creates the potential for Dalmatians to form uratic kidney or bladder stones or other diet-related health problems under certain circumstances. This breed-specific potential for trouble is not, however, a disease; after all, humans have the same potential. Dalmatians simply have an unusual characteristic that must be taken into account by those who want their Dals to live a long and healthy life.

Many of the problems that critics associated with the breed in the 1960s and 1970s were directly related to improper feeding practices common at the time. While veterinary journals described the Dalmatian's metabolism and dietary needs quite adequately, this knowledge had not yet been given mainstream appli-cation. Few people knew which foods were high in purines. Many Dal owners thought overall protein lev-els were the problem, rather than the levels of specific proteins high in purines. Worse, a kind of mistaken, half-true folklore developed concerning the proper feeding of Dalmatians (and misinformation of the half-truth variety is the hardest kind to correct).

Professionals of all categories, including well-respected breeders, veterinarians, and pet food representatives, routinely recommended (and some still do!) products very harmful to a Dalmatian's health. It's no wonder that Dalmatians were not regarded highly by veterinarians. Many dogs had health and temperament problems because they were being systematically, albeit innocently poisoned by their well-meaning, misguided owners.

Over the years, we've experimented with all kinds of dog foods, supplements and combinations of ingredients. We've used canned foods, we've cooked and packaged our own dog food at home, and have come to the educated conclusion that several commercially manufactured dry dog foods work well for Dalmatians.

*Check your
dog's teeth
frequently
and brush
them regularly.*

For the last several years we have successfully fed dry foods with no supplements. It may be hard to find a food that meets the requirements appropriate for a Dalmatian, but if you know what you're looking for, it can be done. We get excellent results with our adult Dals from a dry kibble which is 19 percent protein, corn-based and contains a meat component provided by chicken. We offer it twice daily, preparing it by soaking it in warm water for fifteen minutes before feeding. Our dogs have not had diet-related problems of any kind. It is important to note that in addition to feeding an appropriate food, we ensure that our dogs always have fresh water available and get lots of exercise daily.

Feeding Generalities

Here are some feeding generalities we've learned over the years and recommend for adult Dalmatians:

1. *Never feed a Dalmatian organ meats* such as liver, kidney, sweetbreads or brains in any form, whether cooked, raw or as an ingredient in a pet food or snack.

2. *Never feed a Dalmatian game meat* such as venison or elk in any form, cooked, whether raw or as an ingredient in a pet food or snack.

3. *Never feed a Dalmatian red meat,* cooked or raw, or as an ingredient in a snack or in a pet food *where it appears as one of the first three ingredients listed on the label.*

4. *Never feed poultry* cooked or raw, or as an ingredient in a snack or in a pet food *where it appears as one of the first two ingredients listed on the label.*

5. *Feed most fruits, vegetables and grains* as snacks, *except* those known to be high in purine yields such as *mushrooms, asparagus, legumes, oatmeal, spinach and cauliflower.*

6. *Feed adult Dalmatians pet foods (corn, wheat and rice, in that order) whose protein and fat content are moderate:* about 22 percent protein from low purine sources and no more than 10 percent fat.

7. Fresh water must be available at all times.

8. *Divide the dog's total daily ration into two meals* so that blood levels of uric acid will remain fairly stable. Soak meals in warm water to improve water consumption.

A constant frustration for serious, conscientious breeders is to have their new puppy owners wind up at a pet food store, or even at a veterinarian's office, where they're talked into a "better" kind of dog food than the one the breeder—after years of experience—recommended. Dalmatians are only one of about 140 recognized AKC breeds: because they have different dietary requirements than all the other breeds, it is understandable that the ingredients in premium pet foods are not aimed specifically at keeping Dals fit. What new puppy owners don't know is that pet food representatives do such a good job marketing their products to various pet food outlets, that the store salespeople often become zealots for certain brands, which may very well be outstanding overall but are quite harmful to a Dalmatian.

This caution isn't meant to imply that blind acceptance of breeders' recommendations is necessary or even healthy, either. Breeders *don't* know it all, *and* there are uninformed breeders out there, too. Just remember that if you did your homework to find a good breeder in the first place, don't let the first "pet store nutrition expert" who may have never bred or lived with even one Dalmatian talk you out of that breeder's recommendations. First, check both recommendations against informed veterinary advice. We've included a listing in this chapter of some of the most well-known purine-yielding foods. Compare this against the ingredients listed on dog food labels. Note also that they're like labels for human food: the ingredients are listed from the largest quantity contributors down to the smallest. For instance, a listing of "Corn, Wheat Mill Run, Dried Whole Egg, Chicken Meal," etc., means that corn is the largest constituent in the combination, followed by wheat mill run, dried whole egg, chicken meal, and other ingredients. If a meat product is listed as the first or second ingredient in an adult food, it's been our experience that the food is less suitable for Dalmatians than others that list grains, especially corn, as main ingredients.

FOODS YIELDING HIGH PURINE LEVELS:

Highest
Organ meats
Game meats
Gravies and meat extracts
Canned snack fishes such as sardines and herring
Sweetbreads

High
Meats: beef, veal, pork and lamb
Poultry (poultry is not as high as red meat)
Fish (fresh and saltwater) and shellfish
Oatmeal, whole grains, wheat germ and legumes
Asparagus, cauliflower, mushrooms and spinach

Fruits, nuts and berries
Dairy products
Eggs
Vegetables

If you select your Dalmatian's diet carefully, you will prolong his life and you'll have a healthier dog, too.

Given the higher level of protein consumed by the puppies, it might seem logical to conclude that they should have more energy to burn than the adults. They might be more active, more ready for action, but actually, the energy levels of healthy puppies and adults are about the same. Puppies and youngsters may act goofier, but, pound for pound, they all run at almost equivalent speeds. Adults will hit full physical maturity anywhere from one to three years of age. Our own dogs look like adults at twenty-two months, but will not hit peak development until thirty-four to thirty-six months of age. But they never seem to reach a mental plateau: they're always learning and ready to learn more.

The exuberance of puppies, combined with their running instinct and their affinity for human companionship, can create a formula for trouble if the owner is not careful to monitor how much exercise is prudent for the dog. The Dal is a wonderful jogging companion, but a dog under fifteen months of age has limitations that won't show up in terms of calling it quits. Consider that the Orthopedic Foundation for Animals (OFA) won't accept X rays for hip joint assessment until the dog is two years old, and you begin to realize that there may be hazards in premature extended physical activity.

The best form of exercise for your Dal is the kind it gets on its own. They will find ways to exercise themselves into condition, provided they have appropriate nutrition and a moderate area for movement. They will not, on the their own, extend themselves beyond their endurance or embark on bone-jarring marathons across hard surfaces. They will, however, if they have a master who does those things; they will run themselves into the ground and ask for more.

That's why it's important to start out exercising with the dog in the form of walks and playtime in the park. When you notice that the dog is slowing down, that's about the time you should be walking back up your front steps. It won't take very long for a puppy. Their endurance will grow until the dog reaches fifteen to eighteen months of age. At that time, if you are a runner, you could jog with your Dal until you notice tiring (in the dog, not in yourself). As noted above, a fully mature dog at three years of age will keep up with just about any pace. Still, the dog's condition should determine the extent of the activity, because a healthy Dal will rarely stop (regardless of fatigue or injury) before his master is ready to quit, too. The capacity to stay at this level of activity extends from three to six years, depending on the health and conditioning of the dog. Dals at nine years of age and above are a little choosier about how they spend their energy, if left to their own devices; but they'll still run beyond their limitations if their masters ask it of them.

If you jog or ride a bike and take your Dal with you, use the same common sense you'd use in selecting the best conditions for your own legs and feet. Stay away from concrete and blacktop whenever possible; watch carefully for signs of fatigue, stress, pain or injury; and don't go beyond your dog's capacity.

A FIRST-AID KIT

Keep a canine first-aid kit on hand for general care and emergencies. Check it periodically to make sure liquids haven't spilled or dried up, and replace medications and materials after they're used. Your kit should include:

Activated charcoal tablets

Adhesive tape
(1 and 2 inches wide)

Antibacterial ointment
(for skin and eyes)

Aspirin (buffered or enteric coated, *not* Ibuprofen)

Bandages: Gauze rolls (1 and 2 inches wide) and dressing pads

Cotton balls

Diarrhea medicine

Dosing syringe

Hydrogen peroxide (3%)

Petroleum jelly

Rectal thermometer

Rubber gloves

Rubbing alcohol

Scissors

Tourniquet

Towel

Tweezers

Deafness

Another limiting characteristic encountered in Dalmatians is deafness. Like other white-coated animals (not just purebred dogs, but also randomly-bred dogs, cats, rabbits, mink, mice, etc.), in Dalmatians there is more of a tendency toward deafness than in animals with colored coats. Dalmatian breeders have long recognized deafness as hereditary in their breed because it has always been more prevalent in some lines than others. What breeders lacked was a scientific method by which to limit deafness in their own breeding programs. Then an important piece of the puzzle showed up: several Dalmatian breeders, including Ken Nagler on the East Coast and a veterinarian/breeder named Holly Nelson in Northern California, began a process of dialogue and research that resulted in the discovery that a sizable number of Dalmatians could hear in only one ear.

According to data now collected through a formal program conducted by the Dalmatian Club of America, the incidence of total deafness in Dalmatians (no hearing in either ear) is around 8 percent and the number that hear in only one ear is about 22 percent.

Because deafness in Dalmatians is genetic, regardless of the degree of deafness or whether it occurs in one ear or both, it is a problem that can be minimized by selective breeding. The Dals that carried deafness in only one ear ("unilaterally deaf" Dalmatians) carried the problem forward in the past, before breeders were aware of the phenomenon.

Normal human observation couldn't detect the difference between a Dal with full hearing and one that heard in only one ear: they both acted almost exactly the same. But now, unilateral deafness in Dalmatians is detectable and it is therefore possible to eliminate them from breeding programs, by which the problem could be perpetuated. Today these partially deaf Dals are placed as pets, with breeding restrictions to limit the number of future deaf Dalmatians. These dogs make great pets, because to the pet owner and casual observer, as noted above, their behavior is indistinguishable from a dog with full hearing capacity.

Raising a totally deaf Dalmatian is too difficult for most families, and as a result, deaf Dalmatians who are placed with families often wind up in shelters. That is why thoughtful breeders do not place totally deaf Dalmatians with the public, but instead have them humanely euthanized during the first few weeks of life. Anyone wanting to purchase a Dalmatian should be sure to verify its hearing status very carefully before taking it home. The desire to save a sick, injured or limited animal is natural, but unless a person is extremely unusual and has an equally unusual family, they'll find raising a deaf Dalmatian unbelievably difficult.

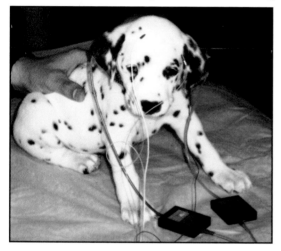

This pup is being BAER-tested for deafness. BAER stands for brainstem auditory evoked response.

Breeders who are working to improve the breed, who want families to enjoy and keep their Dalmatians into old age and who feel responsible for the puppies they place, will not place a deaf Dalmatian. In fact, the Dalmatian Club of America, the AKC parent club for Dalmatians, has a policy that recommends euthanizing deaf Dalmatians. While it may sound heartless, it's a policy with which most breeders eventually agree, and believe to be the most humane course to follow. Breeder responsibility cannot be avoided or passed on. Deafness in the wild is self-limiting.

Skin Problems

One of the Dalmatian's tradeoffs has to do with coat and skin: Because Dalmatians are both short-coated and white-colored, skin problems are immediately apparent. That's good, because the coat and skin are barometers of health; noticing changes early can hasten diagnosis and treatment. It's bad, however, in the sense that the slightest blemish that wouldn't have been seen on a black Labrador, for example, can become a source of concern. With a Dalmatian, it sticks out like a neon sign for everyone to see—and for some to possibly conclude that owning a Dal must mean having to put up with skin and coat problems, or that the owner doesn't really care too much about the condition of his or her dog.

As already noted above, if the nutrition is proper, the chances of running into a serious coat problem are minimized. Some Dals will develop **allergies,** however, that are unrelated to their unique metabolism and which are found among all breeds and mutts. These can arise from inhaled allergens such as pollens and dust, from things in the environment such as wool blankets, or from specific ingredients in food products or chew toys such as wheat or leather. A good veterinary dermatologist is the person to see regarding all skin problems that are of concern to you. Let common sense guide you.

Mothers can pass internal parasites to their babies through their milk.

Parasites such as **fleas** and **mites** can also cause serious skin disorders. Fleas are a problem for all dogs, not only because they make them itch, but also because they are the source of tapeworm infestation. Additionally, some dogs are allergic to them; one flea bite and these dogs get a severe generalized, itchy, reddish reaction. These individuals can be somewhat desensitized by a dermatologist. To eliminate fleas from your dog you must simultaneously eliminate them from his environment.

Flea bombs indoors, yard and kennel sprays outside and flea dips or shampoos and collars for the dog must all be used to have reasonably effective flea control. There are also internal drugs that a veterinarian can prescribe. Ask your veterinarian to put your Dal on a year-round preventive program. And remember, if you have an outdoor cat, you have the potential for constant reinfestation.

Fleas spend only 10 percent of their time dining and dancing on their host. The ones you actually see on your dog are only the ones that are out to feed and mate: multiply the number you find on your dog by ten, and you should be able to figure out roughly how many more are hiding in your house or kennel quarters. And these are only the adults. If you add the eggs, pupae and larvae that are also in the area, you find that adult fleas comprise only 1 percent of the flea population.

FIGHTING FLEAS

Remember, the fleas you see on your dog are only part of the problem—the smallest part! To rid your dog and home of fleas, you need to treat your dog *and* your home. Here's how:

• Identify where your pet(s) sleep. These are "hot spots."

• Clean your pets' bedding regularly by vacuuming and washing.

• Spray "hot spots" with a non-toxic, long-lasting flea larvicide.

• Treat outdoor "hot spots" with insecticide.

• Kill eggs on pets with a product containing insect growth regulators (IGRs).

• Kill fleas on pets per your veterinarian's recommendation.

Research has shown that the adults stay on the ground (or in the carpet) until the shadow of a moving object passes by, whereupon they jump toward the shadow. If they hit, they hang on, feed, breed and hop off. Because dogs are territorial and routine in their travels, it doesn't matter where they hop off, because the dog will invariably pass by again in the future—and they can stay on the ground without another meal anywhere from four months to a year. That's why killing only the fleas that are on the dog or just in his sleeping quarters is not enough. In order to end a flea infestation, you have to take care of all phases of the flea cycle in the entire environment covered by the dog.

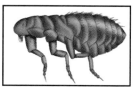

The flea is a die-hard pest.

There are a wide variety of flea killers designed for indoor and outdoor use. Regardless of the specific flea killer used, the house, the dog, the yard and the kennel area all must be treated at the same time, and retreated as flea control directions specify. This is one problem that you can see coming, if you watch for scratching and start searching for fleas in the dog's coat (they all seem to run for the spots, where they become nearly invisible, when you start looking). If you see one flea, it means there are ten adults around. If you have ten adults, you have one thousand in the whole cycle, and you must do something about them. They won't go away on their own.

If you live in a woody, brushy area, you could find ticks as well as fleas on your dog. Ticks, when found, are most commonly seen as pea-sized swollen brown globes. The female attaches to the dog, most often in places that are hard for the dog to self-groom, such as the head, neck, shoulders, ear flaps or between the toes. She sucks blood and swells up to about the size of a pea, mates and then falls off and lays about five thousand eggs.

Ticks carry diseases that are dangerous to dogs and to humans, including Rocky Mountain spotted fever and Lyme disease. If you find one on your dog, it can be removed with a tweezer (not with your fingers—the tick may carry diseases that can infect you), but the

Because of their sensitive skin, Dals need special care to keep them healthy.

most common procedure for removal is to soak them in alcohol or acetone (fingernail polish remover) to kill them, and then pull them out gently with a tweezer. If the head stays on the dog, it should scab over and fall of in a day or so; they rarely get

infected. If you find a large number of ticks, see your vet, as the disease transmission is not the only worry: a heavy infestation can cause paralysis and death.

Mange mites can also do serious damage. Affected dogs look like they scraped off some hair while playing—usually on the head first—rather than looking like they have a skin problem. That the original lesion isn't the result of play becomes apparent only when the scraped-looking area gets bigger. Thirty years ago, few

*These specks in
your dog's fur
mean he has
fleas.*

good treatments for mange existed. Today, veterinarians have an arsenal of drugs, dips and ointments to treat mange, and dogs who are not immune deficient bounce back rapidly. If you suspect mange on your Dalmatian, go to your vet immediately, as it can be quite serious if not treated early. Mange is not a common problem, but if it shows up, it is most likely to become a problem just before sexual maturity.

There are numerous causes for skin and coat problems, but the signals to look for are reddish or burnt-brown hair and reddish skin in the wrinkles of the lower jaw and between the toes; red spots or a reddish hue to the skin in the flank and genital area; reddish irritation between the elbows and the body; red spots or rash along the spinal column; and red spots or a reddish line in the furrow of the topskull. The red-pink coloring and the burnt brown-looking follicular dirt are indications that something is not right; the skin should be white or very light and healthy pink-looking under the hair.

If your Dal rolls over to stretch out in a back massage maneuver, its underside should be blemish-free (no pimples, deposits of fine caked dirt, pustules or irritation marks) and it should be white or light pink. The toes may have some colored hair between them,

*Use tweezers to
remove ticks
from your dog.*

but there is a difference between the normal darker cream to brown discoloration that results from running around, and the reddish-burnt brown and perhaps moist looking appearance of an unhealthy skin and coat.

If you notice that your dog has any of the symptoms mentioned above, a trip to the vet is recommended, and preferably a trip to an experienced canine dermatologist. When the skin and coat get to a point of irritation and infection sufficient to cause the redness noted above, you will probably wind up buying (from the dermatology vet) a shampoo to strip the oils and dirt from the skin and a follow-up shampoo to replace some of the oils. You'll also receive a prescription for a broad-spectrum antibiotic, which is fairly standard treatment and gets rid of the symptoms. It has been our observation, however, that unless the medication continues for at least thirty days, there is a good chance that the skin problem will return. It takes some time for the skin to regenerate itself and for a new, healthy coat to be established.

Food, allergies and parasites have all been noted as culprits in skin problems, but you should also know that the symptoms of skin and coat trouble can be brought on by stress, changing the dog's routine, not having water available, confining the dog in a crate or otherwise restricting the dog's ability to exercise for excessive periods of time.

Ear Care

Regular ear care for any breed of dog is important from a general health and hearing standpoint. With Dals, however, there is an additional care point, common to all breeds of dogs that have fine textured ear leather: you have to watch for skin dryness and possible split ends. Ears commonly produce a small amount of wax. If left unattended, they can also accumulate fine, moist and oily dirt which can in turn serve as a medium for ear mites

---

WHEN TO CALL THE VET

In any emergency situation, you should call your veterinarian immediately. You can make the difference in your dog's life by staying as calm as possible when you call and by giving the doctor or the assistant as much information as possible before you leave for the clinic. That way, the vet will be able to take immediate, specific action to remedy your dog's situation.

Emergencies include acute abdominal pain, suspected poisoning, snakebite, burns, frostbite, shock, dehydration, abnormal vomiting or bleeding, and deep wounds. You are the best judge of your dog's health, as you live with and observe him every day. Don't hesitate to call your veterinarian if you suspect trouble.

or infections of bacteria or yeast, which can all cause ear scratching and head shaking. If neglected ears advance to the stage of head shaking, you run the risk of having your Dal split the end of an ear (when they shake, the ears slap against the top of the head). Once it splits, the wound grows a little larger with each shake. If it gets serious enough, the split ear itself can cause enough irritation to encourage the head shaking.

The end result is an increasing split that starts to bleed and never gets a chance to heal as long as the dog continues to shake its head. And as long as the ear is dirty, infected or irritated inside, the dog will continue to shake. You don't see ears lost to this battle, but you do see Dals that have what looks like a serrated edge on the lower portion of their ear. On rare occasions, you might see one that has a dime-sized portion missing. It's not a hereditary problem. It's almost entirely due to inattention to regular ear care.

If you follow regular ear care, you shouldn't have to worry about ear tips splitting. The good news is that regular ear care is relatively simple and can be done at home with commonly available supplies. The "apple a day" for ears is a quick inspection every week to ten days, backed up by proper maintenance with readily available pet care supplies.

The ears should be pink and clean on the inside and undamaged on the edges on the outside. The best tool for looking into ears is a good quality otoscope. It's like the tool that your family physician uses to

---

IDENTIFYING YOUR DOG

It's a terrible thing to think about, but your dog could somehow, someday, get lost or stolen. How would you get him back? Your best bet would be to have some form of identification on your dog. You can choose from a collar and tags, a tattoo, a microchip or a combination of these three.

Every dog should wear a buckle collar with identification tags. They are the quickest and easiest way for a stranger to identify your dog. It's best to inscribe the tags with your name and phone number; you don't need to include your dog's name.

There are two ways to permanently identify your dog. The first is a tattoo, placed on the inside of your dog's thigh. The tattoo should be your social security number or your dog's AKC registration number.

The second is a microchip, a rice-sized pellet that's inserted under the dog's skin at the base of the neck, between the shoulder blades. When a scanner is passed over the dog, it will beep, notifying the person that the dog has a chip. The scanner will then show a code, identifying the dog. Microchips are becoming more and more popular and are certainly the wave of the future.

*Healthy
Dalmatians are
alert, active
and beautiful.*

examine the insides of your own ears. You can get
them at larger pet shops and through mail order
pet supply catalogs for anywhere from fifteen to fifty
dollars.

The only other things you need as ear care supplies are
cotton balls, gauze or sterile cloth, cotton tipped swabs
and an ear cleaning solution. The ear care products on
the market consist of liquid washes and powders with
cleansing and anti-irritant components. All carry simple cleansing instructions.

EAR-CLEANING RULES

Rule #1. It's always easier to maintain clean ears than to
wait until your Dal tells you that she has an irritation or
infection. These irritations usually stem from bacterial
or yeast infections, so if you see head shaking or ear
scratching with the hind legs, or the kind of foreleg
wiping movement that a dog makes when trying to get
something out of her eye or ear, she probably has more
than debris in the ear.

If you see any of these signs, look inside the ear, use a
liquid ear cleaning solution to wash it out, and blot it
with the cotton. Look inside again to make sure you've
flushed out all of the debris. If you're using a powder
to dry after washing, apply it, but remember the condition of the ear as you last look at it. The next day,

79

look again to see if the dirt production is the same or decreasing, and treat the ear.

Three to five days of treatment should take care of the problem. If it persists longer than that, see a veterinarian. It wouldn't be a bad idea during the course of treatment to rub a small amount of vitamin E oil into the very tip of the ear (the lower end that hangs down by the cheek) to prevent dryness and ear splitting.

If you are lucky enough to catch an ear problem before your Dal splits an ear tip, be sure to keep the dog less active than usual during the course of the treatment. It's not unusual to see them get the bright idea of running out and dive-bombing through loose dirt as a means to scratch their ears after cleaning. Snoods or hoods to cover the ears to prevent ear splitting when head shaking may help, but Dals seem to invent new ways to get rid of hats, clown collars and hoods as quickly as you invent ways to secure them. A watchful, caring eye is once again the most valuable tool in this area of health care. If you let your Dal out after cleaning her ears and she immediately starts shaking, scratching and plowing the ground with her head, it's probably time to consider walking her on a leash for exercise for a day or so until the itch disappears.

This may sound like a lot of attention to a small matter, but ear health is one sign of general health condition. Continuous battles with ear infections could result from poor home health maintenance, but they might also indicate possible low thyroid function or other low-grade infections that generally draw down the vitality and energy of the dog. If you practice regular ear care and your dog still has problems with infections, see a vet, because something else is going on. Check its thyroid levels, blood count and anything else that might have an impact on the general health of your dog.

Treating Split Ears and Tails

If you are unfortunate enough to have to contend with a split ear, the best cure is inactivity. It's the same as if you had chapped lips: don't smile. You can coat the end of the ear with a softening agent, like the vitamin E oil noted above, but the process of healing an ear that slaps against the dog's skull every time it shakes can be a slow one. Some ear splits may be hastened in healing with liquid bandages or hoods. The bottom line, though, is that it will heal faster if the reason for the head-shaking disappears.

This same skin-splitting trouble can arise with the tail of the Dal, too. The same solution applies. You can soften the skin or cover the wound with a liquid bandage (not with a cloth bandage—that will last only about five seconds once you're out of sight), and you must quiet the dog down so she doesn't have the opportunity to bang her tail against anything for awhile. If the dog has sleeping quarters or nesting quarters where it is normally quiet, leave her there except for long walks on a leash—away from objects that she might hit with her tail—for a few days.

From Puppy to Adult

If you obtain your Dal as a puppy, there are a few things to remember that will be health principles throughout her life. All dog health programs have to contend with worms and preventable diseases. So, from the time you pick up your puppy (which should be no earlier than forty-nine days of age) you should pay attention to these details. Your breeder should have taken care of the

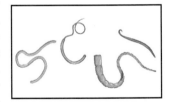

first wormings and shots, and should have a record of what was done. The record should include the dates of medication and vaccination, and should also specify exactly what medicine was used. This information should be given to your veterinarian when you take your puppy in for its first evaluation, immediately after purchase.

Common internal parasites (l-r): roundworm, whipworm, tapeworm, and hookworm.

The thing to know about **roundworms** is that their life cycle almost guarantees that if the bitch has ever had worms in her lifetime, then her offspring will have them, too, because the worms pass from the mother to the puppies before they're born. It's through no fault

81

of the mother or the breeder or the new owner. Even if the bitch is treated for worms before breeding, the treatment only affects worms in the intestinal tract. Those that are in the encrusted stage of the cycle remain unaffected, and still migrate to the puppies when pregnancy occurs.

Puppies should be wormed within the first two weeks after whelping, and examined by a veterinarian for roundworms and other types of worms thereafter. Other types of intestinal worms include **tapeworms, hookworms, whipworms** and **threadworms.** All of these can be detected in stool samples, and all are treatable with a number of deworming agents. **Heartworm** infests the heart (as an adult worm) and the bloodstream (as microfilaria in a live young stage). The heartworm cycle is more complex; it involves mosquitoes as secondary hosts, and is more difficult to treat when an infestation is detected. The most common method of detection is by blood testing for the presence of the microfilaria stage.

Some worming medications can be administered on a monthly basis and will prevent heartworm and some other forms of worms, too. Check with your local veterinarians to find out what is appropriate, and least expensive and best for your dog.

Some types of worms are more common to some sections of the country than to others. The key to knowing what to watch for and what to do is finding a good local veterinarian and becoming a student of animal health care yourself. You should also find out whether there are local breeders who are actively breeding and showing, and who have proven themselves by winning AKC championships and producing championship offspring. You should try to gain permission "to pick their brains." (Always be prepared to bounce the information you get from breeders off the vets, from one vet to another vet, and from one breeder to another. Don't use names and start fights; just play the role of the new kid on the block who is "intelligent enough to understand complex issues but just doesn't know everything yet," and gather information and opinions from as wide a spectrum as possible.)

Vaccines

Even if your breeder takes care of the vaccinations or "puppy shots" and gives you information on what was used and when it was administered, you should still take your puppy to the vet for a checkup and advice on what to do for the remainder of the immunization process. Complete protection usually includes a series of shots through four or five months of age because the puppies carry maternal antibodies (protection from diseases from the mother's own immune system). This maternal protection may interfere with early vaccinations, rendering the puppy unprotected.

The object of vaccination is to cause the immune system to create antibodies to fight a specific disease, so as to have this disease recognition and antibody production available in the event of a real exposure. But if the mother's antibodies do the work for the puppy, then the vaccination is worthless. The mother's protective antibodies gradually disappear. Hence, the most common practice is a series of three shots spaced a month or so apart from eight weeks to five months, depending on the kind of immunization involved.

> **YOUR PUPPY'S VACCINES**
>
> Vaccines are given to prevent your dog from getting an infectious disease like canine distemper or rabies. Vaccines are the ultimate preventive medicine: they're given before your dog ever gets the disease so as to protect him from the disease. That's why it is necessary for your dog to be vaccinated routinely. Puppy vaccines start at eight weeks of age for the five-in-one DHLPP vaccine and are given every three to four weeks until the puppy is sixteen months old. Your veterinarian will put your puppy on a proper schedule and will remind you when to bring in your dog for shots.

Some vaccines carry multiple immunizations, much like measles, mumps and rubella in children's shots. You should note that experimentation has shown that it is wiser to give some forms of immunization separately from others. Ask your vet for details on the current thinking about combining or not combining them, as with coronavirus and parvovirus vaccines in the same immunization, or other combinations that might not be desirable. The final puppy vaccination is usually for rabies, given at six months of age.

Booster shots vary in terms of when they are needed; for example, adult rabies shots are good for three years. Others have different terms of protection. There is a movement afoot in the dog community (as in the human medical community) to look at how much vaccinating we're doing, and what the immunization regime itself does to the dog's health. Implications are being examined for the immune system, reproduction and other areas. Until scientific conclusions are reached, however, the best health care consists of worming, vaccinating, providing a healthy diet, regular grooming practices, watching your dog's attitude and energy level, regular veterinary testing and checkups and following your vet's advice.

General Health and Care Practices

Temperature taking: The most common method for taking a dog's temperature is with a rectal thermometer. As with humans, before you take the temperature, make sure you have a *rectal* thermometer (the oral thermometer has a longer glass bulb on the mercury end; it is not as sturdy in the bulb construction area as the rectal version). Shake the thermometer down below 98 degrees and insert it, bulb end first, about one to three inches, depending on the size of the dog. Hold the dog and the thermometer in place for three minutes. The dog may react by trying to sit down. Make sure that you have control of the thermometer and the dog if he does so. Adult dogs' temperatures normally range from 100 to 102.5 degrees Fahrenheit. The average temperature is 101.3 degrees.

An adult dog's average respiration rate is twenty-two breaths per minute and his heart rate ranges from 60 to 160 beats per minute. The pulse can be taken by placing your hand on the inside of the upper thigh in the area where the thigh joins the body, or by placing your hand on the chest behind the left elbow.

An interesting physiological note, in light of the Dal's peculiar digestive system, is that the daily urine volume per body weight ratio for dogs can be nearly four times that of humans. This fact underscores the importance of having fresh water available to your Dal at all times; of providing frequent opportunities for it to exercise; and of controlling the level of purines in the food you have selected.

This ratio also explains the capacity for frequent urination that dogs, especially males, exhibit. It may be socially inconvenient for you at times, especially if you know that your dog is simply trying to "mark" his territory (remember, they *are* dogs, and the urge is instinctive), but it is also a blessing in that this frequency gives you the opportunity to insure that urination is occurring normally.

In view of the aforementioned uratic stone formation potential, it is important to *notice any irregularity in urination.* If you see your Dal lifting his leg and holding it for longer than usual with no urine stream coming out, it's extremely important to investigate. Note that because of physiology, bitches have far fewer problems with uratic stones than male dogs, and blockage in females is relatively rare. Note also that if urinary tract blockage does occur, it can become life-threatening in a relatively short period of time.

To distinguish urination problems, compare the way a dog normally reacts to new territory: he will investigate it and "mark" it by urinating on two or three or more spots in relatively rapid succession. It's not the same as when the dog gets up in the morning and goes out and empties its bladder. It's a process of lifting his leg to produce a one- or two-second stream of urine to leave his odor on the selected object. If your dog does this at home—that is, goes to several spots in succession and lifts his leg for a moment *and no urine stream is produced,* but only a drop or two comes out, and especially if you know that he would be urinating at that time of day (or it's right after a meal), then you should see a vet. The dog that is trying unsuccessfully to urinate is dangerously close to critical illness.

Of course, if you see any other abnormality such as blood in the urine, darker overall color of urine, or excessive genital-area licking, or notice that the dog is detecting a blood scent on bitches when the bitch is not in season (the dog is attracted to the bitch as if she was in season), it's time to take a trip to the vet.

If your dog has **diarrhea and/or vomits**, both warrant close attention and a possible trip to the vet. Dogs, like humans, will eat things that will cause both conditions. Sometimes they will graze on grass and will cough it back up. Sometimes they will get into material that will give them a loose stool for a day or two. But vomiting and diarrhea can also indicate serious illness or infection.

If your dog goes beyond spitting up grass and throws up an entire meal, and refuses another, it's time to take a temperature and see the vet. If your dog has diarrhea that is nearly liquid, and especially if it carries an acrid odor or shows signs of blood, you should immediately taket the dog to the vet. If you see that your dog has liquid, shooting diarrhea, there is little time to spare. This is especially true if you have a puppy, as dehydration can become critical in an extremely short period of time due to the small body mass of a puppy.

Some of the many household substances harmful to your dog.

If any of the above conditions occur, one of the accompanying signs of distress in your dog can be lethargy and the loss of "sparkle" in the eye. In fact, dogs have a "third eyelid" that normally stays out of sight in good health, but sometimes becomes visible if the dog is ill or upset. It will creep up from the lower portion of the eye and appear as a reddish membrane between the eyelid and the white of the eye. If your Dal is low on energy, something is wrong. Start looking for other signs that could tell you what is going on.

Eye Problems

When eye problems occur, they usually require a trip to the vet. Dogs generally are too fidgety to allow a careful look at the eye, especially if there is an irritation present. If your vet prescribes eye drops or ointment, the administration is different for each kind of medication. Eye drops may be dropped directly into the eye after securing the dog's head, pulling the lower lid down and drawing back on the skin above the eye. Ointment should be squeezed out and placed in the lower lid, not dropped in the eye. The lower lid can then be massaged to spread the oint-ment around.

Squeeze eye oint-ment into the lower lid.

If you see an object floating in the eye which the dog is trying to scratch out, a dampened and flattened cotton swab may be used to pick it out. If the dog is distressed, or if the object is stuck into the eye, or if it is below the third eyelid, see your veterinarian. The dog may have to be anesthetized to safely remove such objects.

Giving a Pill

If you have to give your adult-sized dog a pill, the easiest method is to grasp the muzzle with your left hand (if you're right-handed) from the top, and insert your second and third fingers and your thumb into both sides of the mouth while pushing the

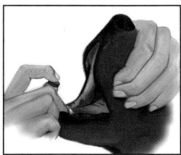

loose skin from the upper jaw into the mouth, using the skin as a pad between your fingers and thumb and the dog's teeth. In this position, the dog will keep his mouth open and, because you have the skin folded over the upper teeth, the dog will not be as eager to close his mouth. After you have the upper jaw held in

To give a pill, open the mouth wide, then drop it in the back of the throat.

this way with your left hand, put the pill as far into the back of the mouth as possible, giving it a push with your index finger to place it almost in the throat. Then remove your right hand quickly, and use both hands to keep the jaws shut, giving only enough freedom to allow the dog to lick his nose. When the tongue comes out for the lick, it means that the dog has swallowed the pill (or has pushed it to the side of the mouth). At that moment, let go of the jaws and watch to see if the dog shakes his head and spits the pill out (sometimes they're pretty clever at this). If no pill is recovered, then you've done your job.

Sometimes it seems almost impossible to get them to swallow and stick their tongue out. If they really resist the pill, covering the end of the nose while you have the jaws shut will also cause them to swallow. By the way, covering a dog's nose in this manner, will also stop a sneezing fit.

If you really have trouble with the dog's oral medication or pills, you may have to disguise the medicine by wrapping it inside a treat or food. Some medications are so bitter that the dog will do almost anything to resist taking them. In cases like these, wrap the pill in a small piece of bread, squeeze the bread until it becomes doughy and cover the entire pill with it. Then take a small amount of crushed kibble and make a slurry out of it, and coat the dough ball pill with the solution. If prepared carefully in this form, the dog will never know what's inside, and the method described above will work.

Most liquid medications are composed with palatability in mind, but some are apparently very bitter. If you are giving a liquid medication and the effort reminds you of giving castor oil to a child, put the liquid in a syringe barrel *with the needle removed,* and open the side of the dog's mouth so that you can get the barrel in near the last molar. Using the jaw-opening method described above, with the fingers cushioned by the lips against the teeth, and with the dog tethered on a grooming stand or to a solid object to prevent wild head swings, position the syringe barrel as far back in the mouth as possible. Squirt the medicine into the back of the throat and hold the jaws shut, covering the dog's nose if necessary until the tongue comes out to indicate that swallowing has occurred.

Emptying Anal Sacs

The only thing that's probably more difficult than giving distasteful medicine to your Dal is expressing anal sacs. If your dog has been confined without the opportunity to exercise at will, as on a long trip, the anal glands could clog up and the sacs could become infected (although this could happen at home, too). The signs of anal sac distress are scooting along the ground and biting at the anal region (these are signs of worms, too, but if you have a regular program of stool sampling and worming, it would be unusual for this to be the cause). Sometimes, with anal sac infections, the tail will hang, as if broken, from about two to three inches from the body. The anal sacs produce a glandular secretion that does not stop when the openings to the sacs become blocked.

The two sacs are located on the lower sides of the anus, on either side, at about the 5:00 and 7:00 positions, and may cause swelling when blocked or infected. They normally feel about the size of two wooden pencils, each about an inch long. When swollen, the "pencils" take on a miniature football shape. Expressing them is a matter of "milking" them from the bottom toward the anal opening, after covering the anus with a tissue (it's impossible to anticipate whether pressure on the sacs will produce a slow release or a spray, and it's also impossible to predict trajectory). The liquid in the sacs is normally gray or brown in color. Because they are scent glands in function, they have a strong odor. If the expressed material is bloody or purulent-looking, see your vet for treatment of a possible infection.

Handling an Injured Dog

If your dog is injured and you don't know the extent of the damage, moving him may be problematic.

Spinal injuries are as delicate a matter in dogs as they are with people who have been in auto wrecks. Slight movement could easily cause more damage. If your dog has been struck and shows signs of moving his hind legs, it's a good sign. In moving the dog, use a board or a blanket; and roll the dog gently onto it,

Make a temporary splint by wrapping the leg in firm casing, then bandaging it.

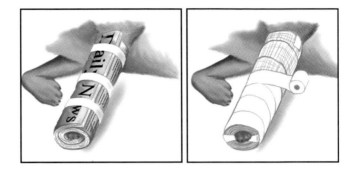

keeping him in the same position as much as possible. Carry him with the help of others on each end of the board or each corner of the blanket if possible. If no one is around and you must move the dog, grasp him behind the hindquarters with one arm and around the front with the other arm, taking care to keep movement at a minimum.

If the dog has an injury that causes **bleeding,** the treatments are the same as for a human. If the bleeding is spurting, it is arterial; if it is a flow, it is venous. Pressure bandaging may stop non-arterial bleeding. It requires putting pressure on the wound until the bleeding stops, dressing the wound by firmly packing it with sterile gauze or a bandage and watching for swelling which might indicate circulation problems. If swelling occurs and it looks like blood pooling beneath the skin, loosen the bandage to allow circulation to the area.

Any **cut** that's more than half an inch in length warrants the attention of a veterinarian, and most likely needs a stitch or two. When a cut stops bleeding, leave it alone. Cleansing a closed wound will only open it up again. If the cut is particularly dirty or the result of a dog bite, see a vet, because antibiotics are certainly necessary.

If an artery is cut and you can't pinpoint it to stop it with your finger or another specific block, a tourniquet may be applied. Apply it between the wound and the heart, loosely wrapping a cloth around the limb and tightening it with a stick until the bleeding stops. A tourniquet must be loosened every half hour for two or three minutes to allow blood to flow to the blocked-off area.

Your dog will not usually bite you if he knows you're helping him, but if an injury occurs, he may not be able to keep from reacting with his teeth to the pain of movement or the trauma of the injury.

In a case where the dog is in pain and reacting defensively, a makeshift **muzzle** can be made out of a strip of cloth or from a leash. Wrap the material from the underside of the jaw to the top of the muzzle, securing it on top with a half-knot. Continue with the material back down to the underside of the jaw and tie another half-knot. From that point, take the ends of the cloth and wrap them around the sides of the neck to the back of the head, where you can tie a square knot to secure and complete the muzzle assembly.

If you happen to see an injury that does not appear to be an emergency, like a cut pad that causes **limping,** it's probably necessary to do nothing more than soak the cut in hydrogen peroxide and let it heal on its own. If you see your Dal limping around for no apparent reason, however, you should thoroughly examine the leg yourself; if you can find nothing, take the dog to the

Use a scarf or hose to make a temporary muzzle, as shown.

vet. The problem becomes *when* to take it to the vet. Dals can play extremely hard, and can sprain a leg or tear a ligament or even break a leg and not register much pain. In fact, dogs that go to veterinarians' offices can produce so much adrenaline that the limps disappear and bone breaks are masked until X-rayed. If your dog comes to the house limping, examine by inspecting for cuts, scratches and scrapes, and by palpating the toes and bone structure up the leg. If no cause is apparent and the limp does not appear to be serious, quiet the dog and watch it. If it's the same or worse after a reasonable rest, take the dog to a veterinarian for a checkup.

Spaying and Neutering

Spaying a bitch is the most common method of removing the possibility of an unplanned pregnancy. It involves surgically removing the uterus, tubes and ovaries. After spaying, the incidence of breast cancer goes down, there is no chance of pyometra, and the bitch will no longer go through oestrous cycles, spotting blood and attracting males twice a year. Most spaying takes place between six months and one year of age. Tubal ligation is also used as a pregnancy control, but in that case, the chances for pyometra still exist, the breast cancer statistics remain the same, and the bitch still attracts males twice annually. Most people prefer the ovary removal as a means of breeding control.

In males, **castration and vasectomy** are used to prevent reproduction. Castration before puberty in males will inhibit certain aspects of growth, so it is advisable to perform this operation after the dog reaches its full growth. A vasectomy also prevents reproduction and does not carry the hazards of disturbing growth that castration does. A vasectomy leaves the male with normal mating urges, but without fertility.

In both males and females, birth control operations have been blamed as causes for weight gain and toning down behavior. But the bottom line of weight gain in most cases is the amount of food and exercise in the dog's routine. As to behavior modification, it's true that the animals won't breed, and, depending on the operation, may have no inclination to do so, but unwanted behaviors are, unfortunately, more frequently related to poor training and owner inattention than physiology.

Spaying and neutering have become more publicized in recent years because of public attention to unwanted animals in shelters. Unplanned litters by non-purebred dogs make up the bulk of the stray and unwanted population, but the issue has affected every purebred breeder in the country. As a result, most pet-quality dogs produced by breeders will only be sold on a spay/neuter contract with a limited AKC registration. The limitation on the registration means that the AKC will recognize the lineage by registration of the animal, but will not register offspring from a dog or bitch carrying a limited registration.

This means of controlling breeding stock improves the chances that knowledgeable breeding will take place, with dogs that will carry the breed forward because of their positive traits and absence of undesirable ones.

A matter of recent public controversy revolves around the contention that purebred-dog genetic factors carry a certain number of physiological flaws and susceptibility to certain diseases. The flames of controversy are fanned by people who ignore the fact that non-purebred animals suffer from the same kinds of conditions, and that there is less attention paid to identifying illnesses and infirmities in non-purebreds and almost none to eliminating them. Purebred-dog breeders, with the American Kennel

---

ADVANTAGES OF SPAY/NEUTER

The greatest advantage of spaying (for females) or neutering (for males) your dog is that you are guaranteed your dog will not produce puppies. There are too many puppies already available for too few homes. There are other advantages as well.

ADVANTAGES OF SPAYING

No messy heats.

No "suitors" howling at your windows or waiting in your yard.

Decreased incidences of pyometra (disease of the uterus) and breast cancer.

ADVANTAGES OF NEUTERING

Lessens male aggressive and territorial behaviors, but doesn't affect the dog's personality. Behaviors are often owner-induced, so neutering is not the only answer, but it is a good start.

Prevents the need to roam in search of bitches in season.

Decreased incidences of urogenital diseases.

Club behind them, have a much better chance of identifying conditions that detract from health and limit lifetimes, and also a much better chance of eliminating the causes.

One of the ways breeders have always had of controlling undesirable breeding is through spaying and neutering. Now, with limited registration, control is more thorough, and because of the political climate, show and breeding stock are more at a premium.

The observations and recommendations in this chapter regarding your Dal's health are by no means the entire story on rearing a long-lived, thriving friend. You can prepare yourself for the task by additional reading and asking of questions whenever you find good sources, but you will discover that your most valuable asset in keeping your Dal in peak condition is your ability to observe and understand what your dog's actions are telling you. Attentiveness is also a key to the next chapter on training, which is both critical and fun if you are to bloom in your relationship with your Dal.

Your Happy, Healthy Pet

Your Dog's Name _____

Name on Your Dog's Pedigree (if your dog has one) _____

_____

Where Your Dog Came From _____

_____

Your Dog's Birthday _____

Your Dog's Veterinarian

    Name _____

    Address _____

    Phone Number_____

    Emergency Number_____

Your Dog's Health

    Vaccines

        type _____ date given _____

        type _____ date given _____

        type _____ date given _____

        type _____ date given _____

    Heartworm

        date tested _____ type used_____ start date _____

Your Dog's License Number_____

Groomer's Name and Number _____

Dogsitter/Walker's Name and Number_____

Awards Your Dog Has Won

    Award _____ date earned _____

    Award _____ date earned _____

part three

Enjoying
your
Dog

chapter 8

Basic
Training

by Ian Dunbar, Ph.D., MRCVS

Training is the jewel in the crown—the most important aspect of doggy husbandry. There is no more important variable influencing dog behavior and temperament than the dog's education: A well-trained, well-behaved and good-natured puppydog is always a joy to live with, but an untrained and uncivilized dog can be a perpetual nightmare. Moreover, deny the dog an education and it will not have the opportunity to fulfill its own canine potential; neither will it have the ability to communicate effectively with its human companions.

Luckily, modern psychological training methods are easy, efficient and effective and, above all, considerably dog-friendly and user-friendly. Doggy education is as simple as it is enjoyable. But before you can have a good time play-training with your new dog, you have to learn what to do and how to do it. There is no bigger variable influencing the success of dog training than the *owner's* experience and expertise. *Before you embark on the dog's education, you must first educate yourself.*

Basic Training for Owners

Ideally, basic owner training should begin well *before* you select your dog. Find out all you can about your chosen breed first, then master rudimentary training and handling skills. If you already have your puppy/dog, owner training is a dire emergency—the clock is running! Especially for puppies, the first few weeks at home are the most important and influential days in the dog's life. Indeed, the cause of most adolescent and adult problems may be traced back to the initial days the pup explores his new home. This is the time to establish the *status quo*—to teach the puppy/dog how you would like him to behave and so prevent otherwise quite predictable problems.

In addition to consulting breeders and breed books such as this one (which understandably have a positive breed bias), seek out as many pet owners with your breed you can find. Good points are obvious. What you want to find out are the breed-specific *problems,* so you can nip them in the bud. In particular, you should talk to owners with *adolescent* dogs and make a list of all anticipated problems. Most important, *test drive* at least half a dozen adolescent and adult dogs of your breed yourself. An eight-week-old puppy is deceptively easy to handle, but she will acquire adult size, speed and strength in just four months, so you should learn now what to prepare for.

Puppy and pet dog training classes offer a convenient venue to locate pet owners and observe dogs in action. For a list of suitable trainers in your area, contact the Association of Pet Dog Trainers (see Chapter 13). You may also begin your basic owner training by observing other owners in class. Watch as many classes and test drive as many dogs as possible. Select an upbeat, dog-friendly, people-friendly, fun-and-games, puppydog pet training class to learn the ropes. Also, watch training videos and read training books (see Chapter 12). You must find out what to do and how to do it *before* you have to do it.

Principles of Training

Most people think training comprises teaching the dog to do things such as sit, speak and roll over, but even a four-week-old pup knows how to do these things already. Instead, the first step in training involves teaching the dog human words for each dog behavior and activity and for each aspect of the dog's environment. That way you, the owner, can more easily participate in the dog's domestic education by directing him to perform specific actions appropriately, that is, at the right time, in the right place, and so on. Training opens communication channels, enabling an educated dog to at least understand the owner's requests.

In addition to teaching a dog *what* we want her to do, it is also necessary to teach her *why* she should do what we ask. Indeed, 95 percent of training revolves around motivating the dog *to want to do* what we want. Dogs often understand what their owners want; they just don't see the point of doing it—especially when the owner's repetitively boring and seemingly senseless instructions are totally at odds with much more pressing and exciting doggy distractions. It is not so much the dog who is being stubborn or dominant; rather, it is the owner who has failed to acknowledge the dog's needs and feelings and to approach training from the dog's point of view.

The Meaning of Instructions

The secret to successful training is learning how to use training lures to predict or prompt specific behaviors—to coax the dog to do what you want *when* you want. Any highly valued object (such as a treat or toy) may be used as a lure, which the dog will follow with his eyes and nose. Moving the lure in specific ways entices the dog to move his nose, head and entire body in specific ways. In fact, by learning the art of manipulating various lures, it is possible to teach the dog to assume virtually any body position and perform any action. Once you have control over the expression of the dog's behaviors and can elicit any body position or behavior at will, you can easily teach the dog to perform on request.

Tell your dog what you want him to do, use a lure to entice him to respond correctly, then profusely praise

Teach your dog words for each activity he needs to know, like down.

and maybe reward him once he performs the desired action. For example, verbally request "Fido, sit!" while you move a squeaky toy upwards and backwards over the dog's muzzle (lure-movement and hand signal), smile knowingly as he looks up (to follow the lure) and sits down (as a result of canine anatomical engineering), then praise him to distraction ("Gooood Fido!"). Squeak the toy, offer a training treat and give your dog and yourself a pat on the back.

Being able to elicit desired responses over and over enables the owner to reward the dog over and over. Consequently, the dog begins to think training is fun. For example, the more the dog is rewarded for sitting, the more she enjoys sitting. Eventually the dog comes to realize that, whereas most sitting is appreciated, sitting immediately upon request usually prompts especially enthusiastic praise and a slew of high-level rewards. The dog begins to sit on cue much of the time, showing that she is starting to grasp the meaning of the owner's verbal request and hand signal.

Why Comply?

Most dogs enjoy initial lure/reward training and are only too happy to comply with their owners' wishes. Unfortunately, repetitive drilling without appreciative feedback tends to diminish the dog's enthusiasm until he eventually fails to see the point of complying anymore. Moreover, as the dog approaches adolescence he becomes more easily distracted as he develops other interests. Lengthy sessions with repetitive exercises tend to bore and demotivate both parties. If it's not fun, the owner doesn't do it and neither does the dog.

Integrate training into your dog's life: The greater number of training sessions each day and the *shorter* they are, the more willingly compliant your dog will become. Make sure to have a short (just a few seconds) training interlude before every enjoyable canine activity. For example, ask your dog to sit to greet people, to sit before you throw his Frisbee, and to sit for his supper. Really, sitting is no different from a canine "please." Also, include numerous short training interludes during every enjoyable canine pastime, for example, when playing with the dog or when he is running in the park. In this fashion, doggy distractions may be effectively converted into rewards for training. Just as all games have rules, fun becomes training . . . and training becomes fun.

Eventually, rewards actually become unnecessary to continue motivating your dog. If trained with consideration and kindness, performing the desired behaviors will become self-rewarding and, in a sense, your dog will motivate himself. Just as it is not necessary to reward a human companion during an enjoyable walk in the park, or following a game of tennis, it is hardly necessary to reward our best friend—the dog—for walking by our side or while playing fetch. Human company during enjoyable activities is reward enough for most dogs.

Even though your dog has become self-motivating, it's still good to praise and pet him a lot and offer rewards once in a while, especially for a good job well done. And if for no other reason, praising and rewarding others is good for the human heart.

To train your dog, you need gentle hands, a loving heart and a good attitude.

Punishment

Without a doubt, lure/reward training is by far the best way to teach: Entice your dog to do what you want and then reward him for doing so. Unfortunately, a human shortcoming is to take the good for granted and to moan and groan at the bad. Specifically, the dog's many good behaviors are ignored while the owner focuses on punishing the dog for making mistakes. In extreme cases, instruction is *limited* to punishing mistakes made by a trainee dog, child, employee or husband, even though it has been proven punishment training is notoriously inefficient and ineffective and is decidedly unfriendly and combative. It teaches the dog that training is a drag, almost as quickly as it teaches the dog to dislike his trainer. Why treat our best friends like our worst enemies?

Punishment training is also much more laborious and time consuming. Whereas it takes only a finite amount of time to teach a dog what to chew, for example, it takes much, much longer to punish the dog for each and every mistake. Remember, *there is only one right way!* So why not teach that right way from the outset?!

To make matters worse, punishment training causes severe lapses in the dog's reliability. Since it is obviously impossible to punish the dog each and every time she misbehaves, the dog quickly learns to distinguish between those times when she must comply (so as to avoid impending punishment) and those times when she need not comply, because punishment is impossible. Such times include when the dog is off leash and only six feet away, when the owner is otherwise engaged (talking to a friend, watching television, taking a shower, tending to the baby or chatting on the telephone), or when the dog is left at home alone.

Instances of misbehavior will be numerous when the owner is away, because even when the dog complied in the owner's looming presence, he did so unwillingly. The dog was forced to act against his will, rather than moulding his will to want to please. Hence, when the owner is absent, not only does the dog know he need not comply, he simply does not want to. Again, the trainee is not a stubborn vindictive beast, but rather the trainer has failed to teach.

Punishment training invariably creates unpredictable Jekyll and Hyde behavior.

Trainer's Tools

Many training books extol the virtues of a vast array of training paraphernalia and electronic and metallic gizmos, most of which are designed for canine restraint, correction and punishment, rather than for actual facilitation of doggy education. In reality, most effective training tools are not found in stores; they come from within ourselves. In addition to a willing dog, all you really need is a functional human brain, gentle hands, a loving heart and a good attitude.

In terms of equipment, all dogs do require a quality buckle collar to sport dog tags and to attach the leash (for safety and to comply with local leash laws). Hollow chewtoys (like Kongs or sterilized longbones) and a dog bed or collapsible crate are a must for housetraining. Three additional tools are required:

1. specific lures (training treats and toys) to predict and prompt specific desired behaviors;

2. rewards (praise, affection, training treats and toys) to reinforce for the dog what a lot of fun it all is; and

3. knowledge—how to convert the dog's favorite activities and games (potential distractions to training) into "life-rewards," which may be employed to facilitate training.

The most powerful of these is *knowledge*. Education is the key! Watch training classes, participate in training classes, watch videos, read books, enjoy playtraining with your dog, and then your dog will say "Please," and your dog will say "Thank you!"

Housetraining

If dogs were left to their own devices, certainly they would chew, dig and bark for entertainment and then no doubt highlight a few areas of their living space with sprinkles of urine, in much the same way we decorate by hanging pictures. Consequently, when we ask a dog to live with us, we must teach him *where* he may dig and perform his toilet duties, *what* he may chew and *when* he may bark. After all, when left at home alone for many hours, we cannot expect the dog to amuse himself by completing crosswords or watching the soaps on TV!

Also, it would be decidedly unfair to keep the house rules a secret from the dog, and then get angry and punish the poor critter for inevitably transgressing rules he did not even know existed. Remember, without adequate education and guidance, the dog will be forced to establish his own rules—doggy rules—that most probably will be at odds with the owner's view of domestic living.

Since most problems develop during the first few days the dog is at home, prospective dog owners must be certain they are quite clear about the principles of housetraining *before* they get a dog. Early misbehaviors quickly become established as the status quo—

becoming firmly entrenched as hard-to-break bad habits, which set the precedent for years to come. Make sure to teach your dog good habits right from the start. Good habits are just as hard to break as bad ones!

Ideally, when a new dog comes home, try to arrange for someone to be present for as much as possible during the first few days (for adult dogs) or weeks for puppies. With only a little forethought, it is surprisingly easy to find a puppy sitter, such as a retired person, who would be willing to eat from your refrigerator and watch your television while keeping an eye on the newcomer to encourage the dog to play with chewtoys and to ensure he goes outside on a regular basis.

POTTY TRAINING

To teach the dog where to relieve himself:

1. never let him make a single mistake;
2. let him know where you want him to go; and
3. handsomely reward him for doing so: "GOOOOOOOD DOG!!!" liver treat, liver treat, liver treat!

PREVENTING MISTAKES

A single mistake is a training disaster, since it heralds many more in future weeks. And each time the dog soils the house, this further reinforces the dog's unfortunate preference for an indoor, carpeted toilet. *Do not let an unhousetrained dog have full run of the house if you are away from home or cannot pay full attention.* Instead, confine the dog to an area where elimination is appropriate, such as an outdoor run or, better still, a small, comfortable indoor kennel with access to an outdoor run. When confined in this manner, most dogs will naturally housetrain themselves.

If that's not possible, confine the dog to an area, such as a utility room, kitchen, basement or garage, where elimination may not be desired in the long run but as an interim measure it is certainly preferable to doing it all around the house. Use newspaper to cover the floor of the dog's day room. The newspaper may be used to soak up the urine and to wrap up and dispose of the feces. Once your dog develops a preferred spot for eliminating, it is only necessary to cover that part of the floor with newspaper. The smaller papered area may then be moved (only a little each day) towards the door to the outside. Thus the dog will develop the tendency to go to the door when he needs to relieve himself.

Never confine an unhousetrained dog to a crate for long periods. Doing so would force the dog to soil the crate and ruin its usefulness as an aid for housetraining (see the following discussion).

The first few weeks at home are the most important and influential in your dog's life.

TEACHING WHERE

In order to teach your dog where you would like her to do her business, you have to be there to direct the proceedings—an obvious, yet often neglected, fact of life. In order to be there to teach the dog *where* to go, you need to know *when* she needs to go. Indeed, the success of housetraining depends on the owner's ability to predict these times. Certainly, a regular feeding schedule will facilitate prediction somewhat, but there is

nothing like "loading the deck" and influencing the timing of the outcome yourself!

Whenever you are at home, make sure the dog is under constant supervision and/or confined to a small area. If already well trained, simply instruct the dog to lie down in his bed or basket. Alternatively, confine the dog to a crate (doggy den) or tie-down (a short, 18-inch lead that can be clipped to an eye hook in the baseboard). Short-term close confinement strongly inhibits urination and defecation, since the dog does not want to soil his sleeping area. Thus, when you release the puppydog each hour, he will definitely need to urinate immediately and defecate every third or fourth hour. Keep the dog confined to his doggy den and take him to his intended toilet area each hour, every hour, and on the hour.

When taking your dog outside, instruct him to sit quietly before opening the door—he will soon learn to sit by the door when he needs to go out!

TEACHING WHY

Being able to predict when the dog needs to go enables the owner to be on the spot to praise and reward the dog. Each hour, hurry the dog to the intended toilet area in the yard, issue the appropriate instruction ("Go pee!" or "Go poop!"), then give the dog three to four minutes to produce. Praise and offer a couple of training treats when successful. The treats are important because many people fail to praise their dogs with feeling . . . and housetraining is hardly the time for understatement. So either loosen up and enthusiastically praise that dog: "Wuzzzer-wuzzer-wuzzer, hoooser good wuffer den? Hoooo went pee for Daddy?" Or say "Good dog!" as best you can and offer the treats for effect.

Following elimination is an ideal time for a spot of playtraining in the yard or house. Also, an empty dog may be allowed greater freedom around the house for the next half hour or so, just as long as you keep an eye out to make sure he does not get into other kinds of mischief. If you are preoccupied and cannot pay full attention, confine the dog to his doggy den once more to enjoy a peaceful snooze or to play with his many chewtoys.

If your dog does not eliminate within the allotted time outside—no biggie! Back to his doggy den, and then try again after another hour.

As I own large dogs, I always feel more relaxed walking an empty dog, knowing that I will not need to finish our stroll weighted down with bags of feces! Beware of falling into the trap of walking the dog to get it to eliminate. The good ol' dog walk is such an enormous highlight in the dog's life that it represents the single biggest potential reward in domestic dogdom. However, when in a hurry, or during inclement weather, many owners abruptly terminate the walk the moment the dog has done its business. This, in effect, severely punishes the dog for doing the right thing, in the right place at the right time. Consequently, many dogs become strongly inhibited from eliminating outdoors because they know it will signal an abrupt end to an otherwise thoroughly enjoyable walk.

Instead, instruct the dog to relieve himself in the yard prior to going for a walk. If you follow the above instructions, most dogs soon learn to eliminate on cue. As soon as the dog eliminates, praise (and offer a treat or two)—"Good dog! Let's go walkies!" Use the walk as a reward for eliminating in the yard. If the dog does not go, put him back in his doggy den and think about a walk later on. You will find with a "No feces–no walk" policy, your dog will become one of the fastest defecators in the business.

If you do not have a back yard, instruct the dog to eliminate right outside your front door prior to the walk. Not only will this facilitate clean up and disposal of the feces in your own trash can but, also, the walk may again be used as a colossal reward.

CHEWING AND BARKING

Short-term close confinement also teaches the dog that occasional quiet moments are a reality of domestic living. Your puppydog is extremely impressionable during his first few weeks at home. Regular confinement at this time soon exerts a calming influence over the dog's personality. Remember, once the dog is housetrained and calmer, there will be a whole lifetime ahead for the dog to enjoy full run of the house and garden. On the other hand, by letting the newcomer have unrestricted access to the entire household and allowing him to run willy-nilly, he will most certainly develop a bunch of behavior problems in short order, no doubt necessitating confinement later in life. It would not be fair to remedially restrain and confine a dog you have trained, through neglect, to run free.

When confining the dog, make sure he always has an impressive array of suitable chewtoys. Kongs and sterilized longbones (both readily available from pet stores) make the best chewtoys, since they are hollow and may be stuffed with treats to heighten the dog's interest. For example, by stuffing the little hole at the top of a Kong with a small piece of freeze-dried liver, the dog will not want to leave it alone.

Remember, treats do not have to be junk food and they certainly should not represent extra calories. Rather, treats should be part of each dog's regular daily diet:

Some food may be served in the dog's bowl for breakfast and dinner, some food may be used as training treats, and some food may be used for stuffing chewtoys. I regularly stuff my dogs' many Kongs with different shaped biscuits and kibble.

Make sure your puppy has suitable chewtoys.

The kibble seems to fall out fairly easily, as do the oval-shaped biscuits, thus rewarding the dog instantaneously for checking out the chewtoys. The bone-shaped biscuits fall out after a while, rewarding the dog for worrying at the chewtoy. But the triangular biscuits never come out. They remain inside the Kong as lures, maintaining the dog's fascination with its chewtoy. To further focus the dog's interest, I always make sure to flavor the triangular biscuits by rubbing them with a little cheese or freeze-dried liver.

If stuffed chewtoys are reserved especially for times the dog is confined, the puppy-dog will soon learn to enjoy quiet moments in her doggy den and she will quickly develop a chewtoy habit—a good habit! This is a simple *passive training* process; all the owner has to do is set up the situation and the dog all but trains herself—easy and effective. Even when the dog is given run of the house, her first inclination will be to indulge her rewarding chewtoy habit rather than destroying less-attractive household articles, such as curtains, carpets, chairs and compact disks. Similarly, a chewtoy chewer will be less inclined to scratch and chew herself excessively. Also, if the dog busies herself as a recreational chewer, she will be less inclined to develop into a recreational barker or digger when left at home alone.

Stuff a number of chewtoys whenever the dog is left confined and remove the extra-special-tasting treats when you return. Your dog will now amuse himself with his chewtoys before falling asleep and then resume playing with his chewtoys when he expects you to return. Since most owner-absent misbehavior happens right after you leave and right before your expected return, your puppydog will now be conveniently preoccupied with his chewtoys at these times.

To teach come, call your dog, open your arms as a welcoming signal, wave a toy or a treat and praise for every step in your direction.

Come and Sit

Most puppies will happily approach virtually anyone, whether called or not; that is, until they collide with adolescence and develop other more important doggy interests, such as sniffing a multiplicity of exquisite odors on the grass. Your mission, Mr. and/or Ms. Owner, is to teach and reward the pup for coming reliably, willingly and happily when called—and you have just three months to get it done. Unless adequately reinforced, your puppy's tendency to approach people will self-destruct by adolescence.

Call your dog ("Fido, come!"), open your arms (and maybe squat down) as a welcoming signal, waggle a treat or toy as a lure, and reward the puppydog when he comes running. Do not wait to praise the dog until he reaches you—he may come 95 percent of the way and then run off after some distraction. Instead, praise the dog's *first* step towards you and continue praising enthusiastically for *every* step he takes in your direction.

When the rapidly approaching puppy dog is three lengths away from impact, instruct him to sit ("Fido, sit!") and hold the lure in front of you in an outstretched hand to prevent him from hitting you mid-chest and knocking you flat on your back! As Fido decelerates to nose the lure, move the treat upwards and backwards just over his muzzle with an upwards motion of your extended arm (palm-upwards). As the dog looks up to follow the lure, he will sit down (if he jumps up, you are holding the lure too high). Praise the dog for sitting. Move backwards and call him again. Repeat this many times over, always praising when Fido comes and sits; on occasion, reward him.

For the first couple of trials, use a training treat both as a lure to entice the dog to come and sit and as a reward for doing so. Thereafter, try to use different items as lures and rewards. For example, lure the dog with a Kong or Frisbee but reward her with a food treat. Or lure the dog with a food treat but pat her and throw a tennis ball as a reward. After just a few repetitions, dispense with the lures and rewards; the dog will begin to respond willingly to your verbal requests and hand signals just for the prospect of praise from your heart and affection from your hands.

Instruct every family member, friend and visitor how to get the dog to come and sit. Invite people over for a series of pooch parties; do not keep the pup a secret— let other people enjoy this puppy, and let the pup enjoy other people. Puppydog parties are not only fun, they easily attract a lot of people to help *you* train *your* dog. Unless you teach your dog *how* to meet people, that is, to sit for greetings, no doubt the dog will resort to jumping up. Then you and the visitors will get annoyed, and the dog will be punished. This is not fair. *Send out those invitations for puppy parties and teach your dog to be mannerly and socially acceptable.*

Even though your dog quickly masters obedient recalls in the house, his reliability may falter when playing in the back yard or local park. Ironically, it is *the owner* who has unintentionally trained the dog *not* to respond in these instances. By allowing the dog to play and run around and otherwise have a good time, but then to call the dog to put him on leash to take him home, the dog quickly learns playing is fun but training is a drag. Thus, playing in the park becomes a severe distraction, which works against training. Bad news!

Instead, whether playing with the dog off leash or on leash, request him to come at frequent intervals— say, every minute or so. On most occasions, praise and pet the dog for a few seconds while he is sitting, then tell him to go play again. For especially fast recalls, offer a couple of training treats and take the time to praise and pet the dog enthusiastically before releasing him. The dog will learn that coming when called is not necessarily the end of the play session, and neither is it the end of the world; rather, it signals an enjoyable, quality time-out with the owner before resuming play once more. In fact, playing in the park now becomes a very effective life-reward, which works to facilitate training by reinforcing each obedient and timely recall. Good news!

Sit, Down, Stand and Rollover

Teaching the dog a variety of body positions is easy for owner and dog, impressive for spectators and extremely useful for all. Using lure-reward techniques, it is possible to train several positions at once to verbal commands or hand signals (which impress the socks off onlookers).

Sit and *down*—the two control commands—prevent or resolve nearly a hundred behavior problems. For example, if the dog happily and obediently sits or lies down when requested, he cannot jump on visitors, dash out the front door, run around and chase its tail, pester other dogs, harass cats or annoy family, friends or strangers. Additionally, "sit" or "down" are better emergency commands for off-leash control.

It is easier to teach and maintain a reliable sit than maintain a reliable recall. *Sit* is the purest and simplest of commands—either the dog is sitting or he is not. If there is any change of circumstances or potential danger in the park, for example, simply instruct the dog to sit. If he sits, you have a number of options: allow the dog to resume playing when he is safe; walk up and put the dog on leash, or call the dog. The dog will be much more likely to come when called if he has already acknowledged his compliance by sitting. If the dog does not sit in the park—train him to!

Stand and *rollover-stay* are the two positions for examining the dog. Your veterinarian will love you to distraction if you take a little time to teach the dog to stand still and roll over and play possum. Also, your vet bills will be smaller. The rollover-stay is an especially useful command and is really just a variation of the down-stay: whereas the dog lies prone in the traditional down, she lies supine in the rollover-stay.

As with teaching come and sit, the training techniques to teach the dog to assume all other body positions on cue are user-friendly and dog-friendly. Simply give the appropriate request, lure the dog into the desired body position using a training treat or toy and then *praise* (and maybe reward) the dog as soon as he complies. Try not to touch the dog to get him to respond. If you teach the dog by guiding him into position, the dog will quickly learn that rump-pressure means sit, for example, but as yet you still have no control over your dog if he is just six feet away. It will still be necessary to teach the dog to sit on request. So do not make training a time-consuming two-step process; instead, teach the dog to sit to a verbal request or hand signal from the outset. Once the dog sits willingly when requested, by all means use your hands to pet the dog when he does so.

To teach *down* when the dog is already sitting, say "Fido, down!," hold the lure in one hand (palm down) and lower that hand to the floor between the dog's forepaws. As the dog lowers his head to follow the lure, slowly move the lure away from the dog just a fraction (in front of his paws). The dog will lie down as he stretches his nose forward to follow the lure. Praise the dog when he does so. If the dog stands up, you pulled the lure away too far and too quickly.

When teaching the dog to lie down from the standing position, say "down" and lower the lure to the floor as before. Once the dog has lowered his forequarters and assumed a play bow, gently and slowly move the lure *towards* the dog between his forelegs. Praise the dog as soon as his rear end plops down.

After just a couple of trials it will be possible to alternate sits and downs and have the dog energetically perform doggy push-ups. Praise the dog a lot, and after half a dozen or so push-ups reward the dog with a training treat or toy. You will notice the more energetically you move your arm—upwards (palm up) to get the dog to sit, and downwards (palm down) to get the dog to lie down—the more energetically the dog responds to your requests. Now try training the dog in silence and you will notice he has also learned to respond to hand signals. Yeah! Not too shabby for the first session.

To teach *stand* from the sitting position, say "Fido, stand," slowly move the lure half a dog-length away from the dog's nose, keeping it at nose level, and praise the dog as he stands to follow the lure. As soon

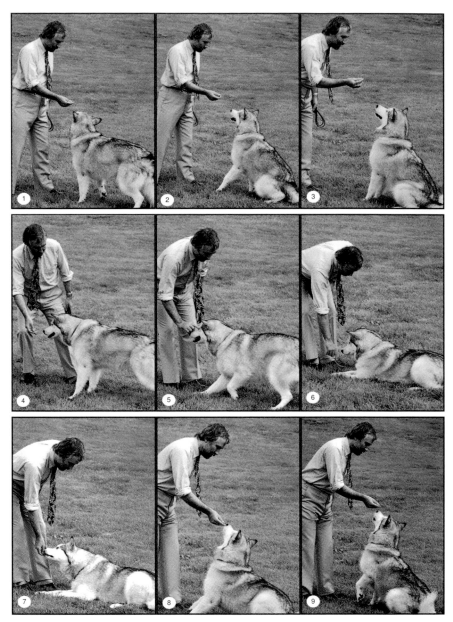

Using a food lure to teach sit, down and stand. 1) "Phoenix, Sit." 2) Hand palm upwards, move lure up and back over dog's muzzle. 3) "Good sit, Phoenix!" 4) "Phoenix, down." 5) Hand palm downwards, move lure down to lie between dog's forepaws. 6) "Phoenix, off. Good down, Phoenix!" 7) "Phoenix, sit!" 8) Palm upwards, move lure up and back, keeping it close to dog's muzzle. 9) "Good sit, Phoenix!"

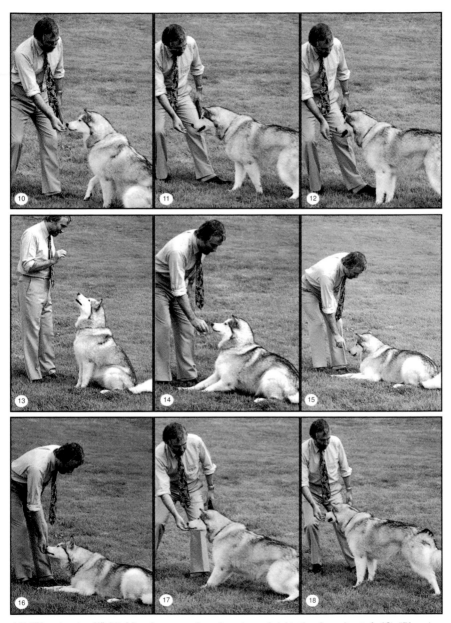

10) *"Phoenix, stand!"* 11) *Move lure away from dog at nose height, then lower it a tad.* 12) *"Phoenix, off! Good stand, Phoenix!"* 13) *"Phoenix, down!"* 14) *Hand palm downwards, move lure down to lie between dog's forepaws.* 15) *"Phoenix, off! Good down-stay, Phoenix!"* 16) *"Phoenix, stand!"* 17) *Move lure away from dog's muzzle up to nose height.* 18) *"Phoenix, off! Good stand-stay, Phoenix. Now we'll make the vet and groomer happy!"*

as the dog stands, lower the lure to just beneath the dog's chin to entice him to look down; otherwise he will stand and then sit immediately. To prompt the dog to stand from the down position, move the lure half a dog-length upwards and away from the dog, holding the lure at standing nose height from the floor.

Teaching *rollover* is best started from the down position, with the dog lying on one side, or at least with both hind legs stretched out on the same side. Say "Fido, bang!" and move the lure backwards and alongside the dog's muzzle to its elbow (on the side of its outstretched hind legs). Once the dog looks to the side and backwards, very slowly move the lure upwards to the dog's shoulder and backbone. Tickling the dog in the goolies (groin area) often invokes a reflex-raising of the hind leg as an appeasement gesture, which facilitates the tendency to roll over. If you move the lure too quickly and the dog jumps into the standing position, have patience and start again. As soon as the dog rolls onto its back, keep the lure stationary and mesmerize the dog with a relaxing tummy rub.

To teach *rollover-stay* when the dog is standing or moving, say "Fido, bang!" and give the appropriate hand signal (with index finger pointed and thumb cocked in true Sam Spade fashion), then in one fluid movement lure him to first lie down and then rollover-stay as above.

Teaching the dog to *stay* in each of the above four positions becomes a piece of cake after first teaching the dog not to worry at the toy or treat training lure. This is best accomplished by hand feeding dinner kibble. Hold a piece of kibble firmly in your hand and softly instruct "Off!" Ignore any licking and slobbering *for however long the dog worries at the treat,* but say "Take it!" and offer the kibble *the instant* the dog breaks contact with his muzzle. Repeat this a few times, and then up the ante and insist the dog remove his muzzle for one whole second before offering the kibble. Then progressively refine your criteria and have the dog not touch your hand (or treat) for longer and longer periods on each trial, such as for two seconds, four seconds, then six, ten, fifteen, twenty, thirty seconds and so on. The dog soon learns: (1) worrying at the treat never gets results, whereas (2) noncontact is often rewarded after a variable time lapse.

Teaching *"Off!"* has many useful applications in its own right. Additionally, instructing the dog not to touch a training lure often produces spontaneous and magical stays. Request the dog to stand-stay, for example, and not to touch the lure. At first set your sights on a short two-second stay before rewarding the dog. (Remember, every long journey begins with a single step.) However, on subsequent trials, gradually and progressively increase the length of stay required to receive a reward. In no time at all your dog will stand calmly for a minute or so.

Relevancy Training

Once you have taught the dog what you expect her to do when requested to come, sit, lie down, stand, rollover and stay, the time is right to teach the dog *why* she should comply with your wishes. The secret is to have many (*many*) extremely short training interludes (two to five seconds each) at numerous (*numerous*) times during the course of the dog's day. Especially work with the dog immediately *before* the dog's good times and *during* the dog's good times. For example, ask your dog to sit and/or lie down each time before opening doors, serving meals, offering treats and tummy rubs; ask the dog to perform a few controlled doggy push-ups before letting her off-leash or throwing a tennis ball; and perhaps request the dog to sit-down-sit-stand-down-stand-rollover before inviting her to cuddle on the couch.

Similarly, request the dog to sit many times during play or on walks, and in no time at all the dog will be only too pleased to follow your instructions because he has learned that a compliant response heralds all sorts of goodies. Basically all you are trying to teach the dog is how to say please: "Please throw the tennis ball. Please may I snuggle on the couch."

Remember, whereas it is important to keep training interludes short, it is equally important to have many short sessions each and every day. The shortest (and most useful) session comprises asking the dog to sit and then go play during a play session. When trained this way, your dog will soon associate training with good times. In fact, the dog may be unable to distinguish between training and good times and, indeed, there should be no distinction. The warped concept that training involves forcing the dog to comply and/or dominating his will is totally at odds with the picture of a truly well-trained dog. In reality, enjoying a game of training with a dog is no different from enjoying a game of backgammon or tennis with a friend; and walking with a dog should be no different from strolling with buddies on the golf course.

Walk by Your Side

Many people attempt to teach a dog to heel by putting him on a leash and physically correcting the dog when he makes mistakes. There are a number of things seriously wrong with this approach, the first being that most people do not want precision heeling; rather, they simply want the dog to follow or walk by their side. Second, when physically restrained during "training," even though the dog may grudgingly mope by your side when "handcuffed" on leash, let's see what happens when he is off leash. History! The dog is in the next county because he never enjoyed walking with you on leash and you have no control over him off leash. So let's just teach the dog off leash from the outset to *want* to walk with us. Third, if the dog has not been trained to heel, it is a trifle hasty to think about punishing the poor dog for making mistakes and breaking heeling rules he didn't even know existed. This is simply not fair! Surely, if the dog had been adequately taught how to heel, he would seldom make mistakes and hence there would be no need to correct the dog. Remember, each mistake and each correction (punishment) advertise the trainer's inadequacy, not the dog's. The dog is not stubborn, he is not stupid and he is not bad. Even if he were, he would still require training, so let's train him properly.

Let's teach the dog to *enjoy* following us and to *want* to walk by our side offleash. Then it will be easier to teach high-precision off-leash heeling patterns if desired. After attaching the leash for safety on outdoor walks, but before going anywhere, it is necessary to teach the dog specifically not to pull. Now it will be much easier to teach on-leash walking and heeling because the dog already wants to walk with you, he is familiar with the desired walking and heeling positions and he knows not to pull.

FOLLOWING

Start by training your dog to follow you. Many puppies will follow if you simply walk away from them and maybe click your fingers or chuckle. Adult dogs may require additional enticement to stimulate them to follow, such as a training lure or, at the very least, a lively trainer. To teach the dog to follow: (1) keep walking and (2) walk away from the dog. If the dog attempts to lead or lag, change pace; slow down if the dog forges too far ahead, but speed up if he lags too far behind. Say "Steady!" or "Easy!" each time before you slow down and "Quickly!" or "Hustle!" each time before you speed up, and the dog will learn to change pace on cue. If the dog lags or leads too far, or if he wanders right or left, simply walk quickly in the opposite direction and maybe even run away from the dog and hide.

Practicing is a lot of fun; you can set up a course in your home, yard or park to do this. Indoors, entice the dog to follow upstairs, into a bedroom, into the bathroom, downstairs, around the living room couch, zigzagging between dining room chairs and into the kitchen for dinner. Outdoors, get the dog to follow around park benches, trees, shrubs and along walkways and lines in the grass. (For safety outdoors, it is advisable to attach a long line on the dog, but never exert corrective tension on the line.)

Remember, following has a lot to do with attitude—*your* attitude! Most probably your dog will *not* want to follow Mr. Grumpy Troll with the personality of wilted lettuce. Lighten up—walk with a jaunty step, whistle a happy tune, sing, skip and tell jokes to your dog and he will be right there by your side.

BY YOUR SIDE

It is smart to train the dog to walk close on one side or the other—either side will do, your choice. When walking, jogging or cycling, it is generally bad news to have the dog suddenly cut in front of you. In fact, I train my dogs to walk "By my side" and "Other side"—both very useful instructions. It is possible to position the dog fairly accurately by looking to the appropriate side and clicking your fingers or slapping your thigh on that side. A precise positioning may be attained by holding a training lure, such as a chewtoy, tennis ball, or food treat. Stop and stand still several times throughout the walk, just as you would when window shopping or meeting a friend. Use the lure to make sure the dog slows down and stays close whenever you stop.

When teaching the dog to heel, we generally want her to sit in heel position when we stop. Teach heel

Using a toy to teach sit-heel-sit sequences: 1) "Phoenix, heel!" Standing still, move lure up and back over dog's muzzle.... 2) To position dog sitting in heel position on your left side. 3) "Phoenix, heel!" wagging lure in left hand. Change lure to right hand in preparation for sit signal.

position at the standstill and the dog will learn that the default heel position is sitting by your side (left or right—your choice, unless you wish to compete in obedience trials, in which case the dog must heel on the left).

Several times a day, stand up and call your dog to come and sit in heel position—"Fido, heel!" For example, instruct the dog to come to heel each time there are commercials on TV, or each time you turn a page of a novel, and the dog will get it in a single evening.

Practice straight-line heeling and turns separately. With the dog sitting at heel, teach him to turn in place. After each quarter-turn, half-turn or full turn in place, lure the dog to sit at heel. Now it's time for short straight-line heeling sequences, no more than a few steps at a time. Always think of heeling in terms of Sit-Heel-Sit sequences—start and end with the dog in position and do your best to keep him there when moving. Progressively increase the number of steps in each sequence. When the dog remains close for 20 yards of straight-line heeling, it is time to add a few turns and then sign up for a happy-heeling obedience class to get some advice from the experts.

4) Use hand signal only to lure dog to sit as you stop. Eventually, dog will sit automatically at heel whenever you stop. 5) "Good dog!"

No Pulling on Leash

You can start teaching your dog not to pull on leash anywhere—in front of the television or outdoors—but regardless of location, you must not take a single step with tension in the leash. For a reason known only to dogs, even just a couple of paces of pulling on leash is intrinsically motivating and diabolically rewarding. Instead, attach the leash to the dog's collar, grasp the other end firmly with both hands held close to your chest, and stand still—do not budge an inch. Have somebody watch you with a stopwatch to time your progress, or else you will never believe this will work and so you will not even try the exercise, and your shoulder and the dog's neck will be traumatized for years to come.

Stand still and wait for the dog to stop pulling, and to sit and/or lie down. All dogs stop pulling and sit eventually. Most take only a couple of minutes; the all-time record is 22 ⅕ minutes. Time how long it takes. Gently praise the dog when he stops pulling, and as soon as he sits, enthusiastically praise the dog and take just one step forwards, then immediately stand still. This single step usually demonstrates the ballistic reinforcing nature of pulling on leash; most dogs explode to the end of the leash, so be prepared for the strain. Stand firm and wait for the dog to sit again. Repeat this half a dozen times and you will probably notice a progressive reduction in the force of the dog's one-step explosions and a radical reduction in the time it takes for the dog to sit each time.

As the dog learns "Sit we go" and "Pull we stop," she will begin to walk forward calmly with each single step and automatically sit when you stop. Now try two steps before you stop. Wooooooo! Scary! When the dog has mastered two steps at a time, try for three. After each success, progressively increase the number of steps in the sequence: try four steps and then six, eight, ten and twenty steps before stopping. Congratulations! You are now walking the dog on leash.

Whenever walking with the dog (off leash or on leash), make sure you stop periodically to practice a few position commands and stays before instructing the dog to "Walk on!" (Remember, you want the dog to be compliant everywhere, not just in the kitchen when his dinner is at hand.) For example, stopping every 25 yards to briefly train the dog amounts to over 200 training interludes within a single three-mile stroll. And each training session is in a different location. You will not believe the improvement within just the first mile of the first walk.

To put it another way, integrating training into a walk offers 200 separate opportunities to use the continuance of the walk as a reward to reinforce the dog's education. Moreover, some training interludes may comprise continuing education for the dog's walking skills: Alternate short periods of the dog walking calmly by your side with periods when the dog is allowed to sniff and investigate the environment. Now sniffing odors on the grass and meeting other dogs become rewards which reinforce the dog's calm and mannerly demeanor. Good Lord! Whatever next? Many enjoyable walks together of course. Happy trails!

THE IMPORTANCE OF TRICKS

Nothing will improve a dog's quality of life better than having a few tricks under its belt. Teaching any trick expands the dog's vocabulary, which facilitates communication and improves the owner's control. Also, specific tricks help prevent and resolve specific behavior problems. For example, by teaching the dog to fetch his toys, the dog learns carrying a toy makes the owner happy and, therefore, will be more likely to chew his toy than other inappropriate items.

More important, teaching tricks prompts owners to lighten up and train with a sunny disposition. Really, tricks should be no different from any other behaviors we put on cue. But they are. When teaching tricks, owners have a much sweeter attitude, which in turn motivates the dog and improves her willingness to comply. The dog feels tricks are a blast, but formal commands are a drag. In fact, tricks are so enjoyable, they may be used as rewards in training by asking the dog to come, sit and down-stay and then rollover for a tummy rub. Go on, try it: Crack a smile and even giggle when the dog promptly and willingly lies down and stays.

Most important, performing tricks prompts onlookers to smile and giggle. Many people are scared of dogs, especially large ones. And nothing can be more off-putting for a dog than to be constantly confronted by strangers who don't like him because of his size or the way he looks. Uneasy people put the dog on edge, causing him to back off and bark, only frightening people all the more. And so a vicious circle develops, with the people's fear fueling the dog's fear *and vice versa*. Instead, tie a pink ribbon to your dog's collar and practice all sorts of tricks on walks and in the park, and you will be pleasantly amazed how it changes people's attitudes toward your friendly dog. The dog's repertoire of tricks is limited only by the trainer's imagination. Below I have described three of my favorites:

SPEAK AND SHUSH

The training sequence involved in teaching a dog to bark on request is no different from that used when training any behavior on cue: request—lure—response—reward. As always, the secret of success lies in finding an effective lure. If the dog always barks at the doorbell, for example, say "Rover, speak!", have an accomplice ring the doorbell, then reward the dog for barking. After a few woofs, ask Rover to "Shush!", waggle a food treat under his nose (to entice him to sniff and thus to shush), praise him when quiet and eventually offer the treat as a reward. Alternate "Speak" and "Shush," progressively increasing the length of shush-time between each barking bout.

PLAYBOW

With the dog standing, say "Bow!" and lower the food lure (palm upwards) to rest between the dog's forepaws. Praise as the dog lowers her forequarters and sternum to the ground (as when teaching the down), but then lure the dog to stand and offer the treat. On successive trials, gradually increase the length of time the dog is required to remain in the playbow posture in order to gain a food reward. If the dog's rear end collapses into a down, say nothing and offer no reward; simply start over.

BE A BEAR

With the dog sitting backed into a corner to prevent him from toppling over backwards, say "Be a Bear!" With bent paw and palm down, raise a lure upwards and backwards along the top of the dog's muzzle. Praise the dog when he sits up on his haunches and offer the treat as a reward. To prevent the dog from standing on his hind legs, keep the lure closer to the dog's muzzle. On each trial, progressively increase the length of time the dog is required to sit up to receive a food reward. Since lure/reward training is so easy, teach the dog to stand and walk on his hind legs as well!

Teaching "Be a Bear"

Getting
Active
with your Dog

by Bardi McLennan

Once you and your dog have graduated from basic obedience training and are beginning to work together as a team, you can take part in the growing world of dog activities. There are so many fun things to do with your dog! Just remember, people and dogs don't always learn at the same pace, so don't be upset if you (or your dog) need more than two basic training courses before your team becomes operational. Even smart dogs don't go straight to college from kindergarten!

Just as there are events geared to certain types of dogs, so there are ones that are more appealing to certain types of people. In some activities, you give the commands and your dog does the work (upland game hunting is one example), while in others, such as agility, you'll both get a workout. You may want to aim for prestigious titles to add to your dog's name, or you may want nothing more than the sheer enjoyment of being around other people and their dogs. Passive or active, participation has its own rewards.

Consider your dog's physical capabilities when looking into any of the canine activities. It's easy to see that a Basset Hound is not built for the racetrack, nor would a Chihuahua be the breed of choice for pulling a sled. A loyal dog will attempt almost anything you ask him to do, so it is up to you to know your

All dogs seem to love playing flyball.

dog's limitations. A dog must be physically sound in order to compete at any level in athletic activities, and being mentally sound is a definite plus. Advanced age, however, may not be a deterrent. Many dogs still hunt and herd at ten or twelve years of age. It's entirely possible for dogs to be "fit at 50." Take your dog for a checkup, explain to your vet the type of activity you have in mind and be guided by his or her findings.

You needn't be restricted to breed-specific sports if it's only fun you're after. Certain AKC activities are limited to designated breeds; however, as each new trial, test or sport has grown in popularity, so has the variety of breeds encouraged to participate at a fun level.

But don't shortchange your fun, or that of your dog, by thinking only of the basic function of her breed. Once a dog has learned how to learn, she can be taught to do just about anything as long as the size of the dog is right for the job and you both think it is fun and rewarding. In other words, you are a team.

To get involved in any of the activities detailed in this chapter, look for the names and addresses of the organizations that sponsor them in Chapter 13. You can also ask your breeder or a local dog trainer for contacts.

Official American Kennel Club Activities

The following tests and trials are some of the events sanctioned by the AKC and sponsored by various dog clubs. Your dog's expertise will be rewarded with impressive titles. You can participate just for fun, or be competitive and go for those awards.

OBEDIENCE

Training classes begin with pups as young as three months of age in kindergarten puppy training,

You can compete in obedience trials with a well trained dog.

then advance to pre-novice (all exercises on lead) and go on to novice, which is where you'll start off-lead work. In obedience classes dogs learn to sit, stay, heel and come through a variety of exercises. Once you've got the basics down, you can enter obedience trials and work toward earning your dog's first degree, a C.D. (Companion Dog).

The next level is called "Open," in which jumps and retrieves perk up the dog's interest. Passing grades in competition at this level earn a C.D.X. (Companion Dog Excellent). Beyond that lies the goal of the most ambitious—Utility (U.D. and even U.D.X. or OTCh, an Obedience Champion).

AGILITY

All dogs can participate in the latest canine sport to have gained worldwide popularity for its fun and excitement, agility. It began in England as a canine version of horse show-jumping, but because dogs are more agile and able to perform on verbal commands, extra feats were added such as climbing, balancing and racing through tunnels or in and out of weave poles. Many of the obstacles (regulation or homemade) can be set up in your own backyard. If the agility bug bites, you could end up in international competition!

For starters, your dog should be obedience trained, even though, in the beginning, the lessons may all be taught on lead. Once the dog understands the commands (and you do, too), it's as easy as guiding the dog over a prescribed course, one obstacle at a time. In competition, the race is against the clock, so wear your running shoes! The dog starts with 200 points and the judge deducts for infractions and misadventures along the way.

All dogs seem to love agility and respond to it as if they were being turned loose in a playground paradise. Your dog's enthusiasm will be contagious; agility turns into great fun for dog and owner.

FIELD TRIALS AND HUNTING TESTS

There are field trials and hunting tests for the sporting breeds—retrievers, spaniels and pointing breeds, and for some hounds—Bassets, Beagles and Dachshunds. Field trials are competitive events that test a dog's ability to perform the functions for which she was bred. Hunting tests, which are open to retrievers,

---

TITLES AWARDED BY THE AKC

Conformation: Ch. (Champion)

Obedience: CD (Companion Dog); CDX (Companion Dog Excellent); UD (Utility Dog); UDX (Utility Dog Excellent); OTCh. (Obedience Trial Champion)

Field: JH (Junior Hunter); SH (Senior Hunter); MH (Master Hunter); AFCh. (Amateur Field Champion); FCh. (Field Champion)

Lure Coursing: JC (Junior Courser); SC (Senior Courser)

Herding: HT (Herding Tested); PT (Pre-Trial Tested); HS (Herding Started); HI (Herding Intermediate); HX (Herding Excellent); HCh. (Herding Champion)

Tracking: TD (Tracking Dog); TDX (Tracking Dog Excellent)

Agility: NAD (Novice Agility); OAD (Open Agility); ADX (Agility Excellent); MAX (Master Agility)

Earthdog Tests: JE (Junior Earthdog); SE (Senior Earthdog); ME (Master Earthdog)

Canine Good Citizen: CGC

Combination: DC (Dual Champion—Ch. and Fch.); TC (Triple Champion—Ch., Fch., and OTCh.)

spaniels and pointing breeds only, are noncompetitive and are a means of judging the dog's ability as well as that of the handler.

Hunting is a very large and complex part of canine sports, and if you own one of the breeds that hunts, the events are a great treat for your dog and you. He gets to do what he was bred for, and you get to work with him and watch him do it. You'll be proud of and amazed at what your dog can do.

Fortunately, the AKC publishes a series of booklets on these events, which outline the rules and regulations and include a glossary of the sometimes complicated terms. The AKC also publishes newsletters for field trialers and hunting test enthusiasts. The United Kennel Club (UKC) also has informative materials for the hunter and his dog.

Retrievers and other sporting breeds get to do what they're bred to in hunting tests.

HERDING TESTS AND TRIALS

Herding, like hunting, dates back to the first known uses man made of dogs. The interest in herding today is widespread, and if you own a herding breed, you can join in the activity. Herding dogs are tested for their natural skills to keep a flock of ducks, sheep or cattle together. If your dog shows potential, you can start at the testing level, where your dog can earn a title for showing an inherent herding ability. With training you can advance to the trial level, where your dog should be capable of controlling even difficult livestock in diverse situations.

LURE COURSING

The AKC Tests and Trials for Lure Coursing are open to traditional sighthounds—Greyhounds, Whippets,

Borzoi, Salukis, Afghan Hounds, Ibizan Hounds and Scottish Deerhounds—as well as to Basenjis and Rhodesian Ridgebacks. Hounds are judged on overall ability, follow, speed, agility and endurance. This is possibly the most exciting of the trials for spectators, because the speed and agility of the dogs is awesome to watch as they chase the lure (or "course") in heats of two or three dogs at a time.

TRACKING

Tracking is another activity in which almost any dog can compete because every dog that sniffs the ground when taken outdoors is, in fact, tracking. The hard part comes when the rules as to what, when and where the dog tracks are determined by a person, not the dog! Tracking tests cover a large area of fields, woods and roads. The tracks are laid hours before the dogs go to work on them, and include "tricks" like cross-tracks and sharp turns. If you're interested in search-and-rescue work, this is the place to start.

This tracking dog is hot on the trail.

EARTHDOG TESTS FOR SMALL TERRIERS AND DACHSHUNDS

These tests are open to Australian, Bedlington, Border, Cairn, Dandie Dinmont, Smooth and Wire Fox, Lakeland, Norfolk, Norwich, Scottish, Sealyham, Skye, Welsh and West Highland White Terriers as well as Dachshunds. The dogs need no prior training for this terrier sport. There is a qualifying test on the day of the event, so dog and handler learn the rules on the spot. These tests, or "digs," sometimes end with informal races in the late afternoon.

Here are some of the extracurricular obedience and racing activities that are not regulated by the AKC or UKC, but are generally run by clubs or a group of dog fanciers and are often open to all.

Canine Freestyle This activity is something new on the scene and is variously likened to dancing, dressage or ice skating. It is meant to show the athleticism of the dog, but also requires showmanship on the part of the dog's handler. If you and your dog like to ham it up for friends, you might want to look into freestyle.

Lure coursing lets sighthounds do what they do best—run!

Scent Hurdle Racing Scent hurdle racing is purely a fun activity sponsored by obedience clubs with members forming competing teams. The height of the hurdles is based on the size of the shortest dog on the team. On a signal, one team dog is released on each of two side-by-side courses and must clear every hurdle before picking up its own dumbbell from a platform and returning over the jumps to the handler. As each dog returns, the next on that team is sent. Of course, that is what the dogs are supposed to do. When the dogs improvise (going under or around the hurdles, stealing another dog's dumbbell, and so forth), it no doubt frustrates the handlers, but just adds to the fun for everyone else.

Flyball This type of racing is similar, but after negotiating the four hurdles, the dog comes to a flyball box, steps on a lever that releases a tennis ball into the air, catches the ball and returns over the hurdles to the starting point. This game also becomes extremely fun for spectators because the dogs sometimes cheat by catching a ball released by the dog in the next lane. Three titles can be earned—Flyball Dog (F.D.), Flyball Dog Excellent (F.D.X.) and Flyball Dog Champion (Fb.D.Ch.)—all awarded by the North American Flyball Association, Inc.

Dogsledding The name conjures up the Rocky Mountains or the frigid North, but you can find dogsled clubs in such unlikely spots as Maryland, North Carolina and Virginia! Dogsledding is primarily for the Nordic breeds such as the Alaskan Malamutes, Siberian Huskies and Samoyeds, but other breeds can try. There are some practical backyard applications to this sport, too. With parental supervision, almost any strong dog could pull a child's sled.

Coming over the A-frame on an agility course.

These are just some of the many recreational ways you can get to know and understand your multifaceted dog better and have fun doing it.

chapter 10

Your Dog
and your
Family

by Bardi McLennan

Adding a dog automatically increases your family by one, no matter whether you live alone in an apartment or are part of a mother, father and six kids household. The single-person family is fair game for numerous and varied canine misconceptions as to who is dog and who pays the bills, whereas a dog in a houseful of children will consider himself to be just one of the gang, littermates all. One dog and one child may give a dog reason to believe they are both kids or both dogs.

Either interpretation requires parental supervision and sometimes speedy intervention.

As soon as one paw goes through the door into your home, Rufus (or Rufina) has to make many adjustments to become a part of your family. Your job is to make him fit in as painlessly as possible. An older dog may have some frame of reference from past experience, but to a 10-week-old puppy, everything is brand new: people, furniture, stairs, when and where people eat, sleep or watch TV, his own place and everyone else's space, smells, sounds, outdoors—everything!

Puppies, and newly acquired dogs of any age, do not need what we think of as "freedom." If you leave a new dog or puppy loose in the house, you will almost certainly return to chaotic destruction and the dog will forever after equate your homecoming with a time of punishment to be dreaded. It is unfair to give your dog what amounts to "freedom to get into trouble." Instead, confine him to a crate for brief periods of your absence (up to three or four hours) and, for the long haul, a workday for example, confine him to one untrashable area with his own toys, a bowl of water and a radio left on (low) in another room.

Lots of pets get along with each other just fine.

For the first few days, when not confined, put Rufus on a long leash tied to your wrist or waist. This umbilical cord method enables the dog to learn all about you from your body language and voice, and to learn by his own actions which things in the house are NO! and which ones are rewarded by "Good dog." Housetraining will be easier with the pup always by your side. Speaking of which, accidents do happen. That goal of "completely housetrained" takes up to a year, or the length of time it takes the pup to mature.

The All-Adult Family

Most dogs in an adults-only household today are likely to be latchkey pets, with no one home all day but the dog. When you return after a tough day on the job, the dog can and should be your relaxation therapy. But going home can instead be a daily frustration.

Separation anxiety is a very common problem for the dog in a working household. It may begin with whines and barks of loneliness, but it will soon escalate into a frenzied destruction derby. That is why it is so important to set aside the time to teach a dog to relax when left alone in his confined area and to understand that he can trust you to return.

Let the dog get used to your work schedule in easy stages. Confine him to one room and go in and out of that room over and over again. Be casual about it. No physical, voice or eye contact. When the pup no longer even notices your comings and goings, leave the house for varying lengths of time, returning to stay home for a few minutes and gradually increasing the time away. This training can take days, but the dog is learning that you haven't left him forever and that he can trust you.

Any time you leave the dog, but especially during this training period, be casual about your departure. No anxiety-building fond farewells. Just "Bye" and go! Remember the "Good dog" when you return to find everything more or less as you left it.

If things are a mess (or even a disaster) when you return, greet the dog, take him outside to eliminate, and then put him in his crate while you clean up. Rant and rave in the shower! *Do not* punish the dog. You were not there when it happened, and the rule is: Only punish as you catch the dog in the act of wrongdoing. Obviously, it makes sense to get your latchkey puppy when you'll have a week or two to spend on these training essentials.

Family weekend activities should include Rufus whenever possible. Depending on the pup's age, now is the time for a long walk in the park, playtime in the backyard, a hike in the woods. Socializing is as important as health care, good food and physical exercise, so visiting Aunt Emma or Uncle Harry and the next-door neighbor's dog or cat is essential to developing an out-going, friendly temperament in your pet.

If you are a single adult, socializing Rufus at home and away will prevent him from becoming overly protective of you (or just overly attached) and will also prevent such behavioral problems as dominance or fear of strangers.

Babies

Whether already here or on the way, babies figure larger than life in the eyes of a dog. If the dog is there first, let him in on all your baby preparations in the house. When baby arrives, let Rufus sniff any item of clothing that has been on the baby before Junior comes home. Then let Mom greet the dog first before introducing the new family member. Hold the baby down for the dog to see and sniff, but make sure some-one's holding the dog on lead in case of any sudden moves. Don't play keep-away or tease the dog with the baby, which only invites undesirable jump-ing up.

The dog and the baby are "family," and for starters can be treated almost as equals. Things rapidly change, however, espe-cially when baby takes to creeping around on all fours on the dog's turf or, better yet, has yummy pudding all over her face and hands! That's when a lot of things in the dog's and baby's lives become more separate than equal.

Dogs are perfect confidants.

Toddlers make terrible dog owners, but if you can't avoid the combination, use patient discipline (that is, positive teaching rather than punishment), and use time-outs before you run out of patience.

A dog and a baby (or toddler, or an assertive young child) should never be left alone together. Take the dog with you or confine him. With a baby or youngsters in the house, you'll have plenty of use for that wonderful canine safety device called a crate!

Young Children

Any dog in a house with kids will behave pretty much as the kids do, good or bad. But even good dogs and good children can get into trouble when play becomes rowdy and active.

Teach children how to play nicely with a puppy.

Legs bobbing up and down, shrill voices screeching, a ball hurtling overhead, all add up to exuberant frustration for a dog who's just trying to be part of the gang. In a pack of puppies, any legs or toys being chased would be caught by a set of teeth, and all the pups involved would understand that is how the game is played. Kids do not understand this, nor do parents tolerate it. Bring Rufus indoors before you have reason to regret it. This is time-out, not a punishment.

You can explain the situation to the children and tell them they must play quieter games until the puppy learns not to grab them with his mouth. Unfortunately, you can't explain it that easily to the dog. With adult supervision, they will learn how to play together.

Young children love to tease. Sticking their faces or wiggling their hands or fingers in the dog's face is teasing. To another person it might be just annoying, but it is threatening to a dog. There's another difference: We can make the child stop by an explanation, but the only way a dog can stop it is with a warning growl and then with teeth. Teasing is the major cause of children being bitten by their pets. Treat it seriously.

Older Children

The best age for a child to get a first dog is between the ages of 8 and 12. That's when kids are able to accept some real responsibility for their pet. Even so, take the child's vow of "I will never *ever* forget to feed (brush, walk, etc.) the dog" for what it's worth: a child's good intention at that moment. Most kids today have extra lessons, soccer practice, Little League, ballet, and so forth piled on top of school schedules. There will be many times when Mom will have to come to the dog's rescue. "I walked the dog for you so you can set the table for me" is one way to get around a missed appointment without laying on blame or guilt.

Kids in this age group make excellent obedience trainers because they are into the teaching/learning process themselves and they lack the self-consciousness of adults. Attending a dog show is something the whole family can enjoy, and watching Junior Showmanship may catch the eye of the kids. Older children can begin to get involved in many of the recreational activities that were reviewed in the previous chapter. Some of the agility obstacles, for example, can be set up in the backyard as a family project (with an adult making sure all the equipment is safe and secure for the dog).

Older kids are also beginning to look to the future, and may envision themselves as veterinarians or trainers or show dog handlers or writers of the next Lassie best-seller. Dogs are perfect confidants for these dreams. They won't tell a soul.

Other Pets

Introduce all pets tactfully. In a dog/cat situation, hold the dog, not the cat. Let two dogs meet on neutral turf—a stroll in the park or a walk down the street— with both on loose leads to permit all the normal canine ways of saying hello, including routine sniffing, circling, more sniffing, and so on. Small creatures such as hamsters, chinchillas or mice must be kept safe from their natural predators (dogs and cats).

Festive Family Occasions

Parties are great for people, but not necessarily for puppies. Until all the guests have arrived, put the dog in his crate or in a room where he won't be disturbed. A socialized dog can join the fun later as long as he's not underfoot, annoying guests or into the hors d'oeuvres.

There are a few dangers to consider, too. Doors opening and closing can allow a puppy to slip out unnoticed in the confusion, and you'll be organizing a search party instead of playing host or hostess. Party food and buffet service are not for dogs. Let Rufus party in his crate with a nice big dog biscuit.

At Christmas time, not only are tree decorations dangerous and breakable (and perhaps family heirlooms), but extreme caution should be taken with the lights, cords and outlets for the tree lights and any other festive lighting. Occasionally a dog lifts a leg, ignoring the fact that the tree is indoors. To avoid this, use a canine repellent, made for gardens, on the tree. Or keep him out of the tree room unless supervised. And whatever you do, *don't* invite trouble by hanging his toys on the tree!

Car Travel

Before you plan a vacation by car or RV with Rufus, be sure he enjoys car travel. Nothing spoils a holiday quicker than a carsick dog! Work within the dog's comfort level. Get in the car with the dog in his crate or attached to a canine car safety belt and just sit there until he relaxes. That's all. Next time, get in the car, turn on the engine and go nowhere. Just sit. When that is okay, turn on the engine and go around the block. Now you can go for a ride and include a stop where you get out, leaving the dog for a minute or two.

On a warm day, always park in the shade and leave windows open several inches. And return quickly. It only takes 10 minutes for a car to become an overheated steel death trap.

Motel or Pet Motel?

Not all motels or hotels accept pets, but you have a much better choice today than even a few years ago. To find a dog-friendly lodging, look at *On the Road Again With Man's Best Friend*, a series of directories that detail bed and breakfasts, inns, family resorts and other hotels/motels. Some places require a refundable deposit to cover any damage incurred by the dog. More B&Bs accept pets now, but some restrict the size.

If taking Rufus with you is not feasible, check out boarding kennels in your area. Your veterinarian may offer this service, or recommend a kennel or two he or she is familiar with. Go see the facilities for yourself, ask about exercise, diet, housing, and so on. Or, if you'd rather have Rufus stay home, look into bonded petsitters, many of whom will also bring in the mail and water your plants.

chapter 11

Your Dog
and your
Community

by Bardi McLennan

Step outside your home with your dog and you are no longer just family, you are both part of your community. This is when the phrase "responsible pet ownership" takes on serious implications. For starters, it means you pick up after your dog—not just occasionally, but every time your dog eliminates away from home. That means you have joined the Plastic Baggy Brigade! You always have plastic sandwich bags in your pocket and several in the car. It means you teach your kids how to use them, too. If you think this is "yucky," just imagine what

the person (a non-doggy person) who inadvertently steps in the mess thinks!

Your responsibility extends to your neighbors: To their ears (no annoying barking); to their property (their garbage, their lawn, their flower beds, their cat—especially their cat); to their kids (on bikes, at play); to their kids' toys and sports equipment.

There are numerous dog-related laws, ranging from simple dog licensing and leash laws to those holding you liable for any physical injury or property damage done by your dog. These laws are in place to protect everyone in the community, including you and your dog. There are town ordinances and state laws which are by no means the same in all towns or all states. Ignorance of the law won't get you off the hook. The time to find out what the laws are where you live is now.

Be sure your dog's license is current. This is not just a good local ordinance, it can make the difference between finding your lost dog or not. Many states now require proof of rabies vaccination and that the dog has been spayed or neutered before issuing a license. At the same time, keep up the dog's annual immunizations.

Dressing your dog up makes him appealing to strangers.

Never let your dog run loose in the neighborhood. This will not only keep you on the right side of the leash law, it's the outdoor version of the rule about not giving your dog "freedom to get into trouble."

Good Canine Citizen

Sometimes it's hard for a dog's owner to assess whether or not the dog is sufficiently socialized to be accepted by the community at large. Does Rufus or Rufina display good, controlled behavior in public? The AKC's Canine Good Citizen program is available through many dog organizations. If your dog passes the test, the title "CGC" is earned.

The overall purpose is to turn your dog into a good neighbor and to teach you about your responsibility to your community as a dog owner. Here are the ten things your dog must do willingly:

1. Allow a stranger to handle him or her as a groomer or veterinarian would.
2. Accept a stranger stopping to chat with you.
3. Walk nicely on a loose lead.
4. Walk calmly through a crowd.
5. Sit and be petted by a stranger.
6. Sit and down on command.
7. Stay put when you move away.
8. Casually greet another dog.
9. React confidently to distractions.
10. Accept being tied up in a strange place and left alone for a few minutes.

Schools and Dogs

Schools are getting involved with pet ownership on an educational level. It has been proven that children who are kind to animals are humane in their attitude toward other people as adults.

A dog is a child's best friend, and so children are often primary pet owners, if not the primary caregivers. Unfortunately, they are also the ones most often bitten by dogs. This occurs due to a lack of understanding that pets, no matter how sweet, cuddly and loving, are still animals. Schools, along with parents, dog clubs, dog fanciers and the AKC, are working to change all that with video programs for children not only in grade school, but in the nursery school and pre-kindergarten age group. Teaching youngsters how to be responsible dog owners is important community work. When your dog has a CGC, volunteer to take part in an educational classroom event put on by your dog club.

Boy Scout Merit Badge

A Merit Badge for Dog Care can be earned by any Boy Scout ages 11 to 18. The requirements are not easy, but amount to a complete course in responsible dog care and general ownership. Here are just a few of the things a Scout must do to earn that badge:

> Point out ten parts of the dog using the correct names.

> Give a report (signed by parent or guardian) on your care of the dog (feeding, food used, housing, exercising, grooming and bathing), plus what has been done to keep the dog healthy.

> Explain the right way to obedience train a dog, and demonstrate three comments.

> Several of the requirements have to do with health care, including first aid, handling a hurt dog, and the dangers of home treatment for a serious ailment.

> The final requirement is to know the local laws and ordinances involving dogs.

There are similar programs for Girl Scouts and 4-H members.

Local Clubs

Local dog clubs are no longer in existence just to put on a yearly dog show. Today, they are apt to be the hub of the community's involvement with pets. Dog clubs conduct educational forums with big-name speakers, stage demonstrations of canine talent in a busy mall and take dogs of various breeds to schools for class-room discussion.

The quickest way to feel accepted as a member in a club is to volunteer your services! Offer to help with something—anything—and watch your popularity (and your interest) grow.

Therapy Dogs

Once your dog has earned that essential CGC and reliably demonstrates a steady, calm temperament, you could look into what therapy dogs are doing in your area.

Therapy dogs go with their owners to visit patients at hospitals or nursing homes, generally remaining on leash but able to coax a pat from a stiffened hand, a smile from a blank face, a few words from sealed lips or a hug from someone in need of love.

Nursing homes cover a wide range of patient care. Some specialize in care of the elderly, some in the treatment of specific illnesses, some in physical therapy. Children's facilities also welcome visits from trained therapy dogs for boosting morale in their pediatric patients. Hospice care for the terminally ill and the at-home care of AIDS patients are other areas where this canine visiting is desperately needed. Therapy dog training comes first.

Your dog can make a differ-ence in lots of lives.

There is a lot more involved than just taking your nice friendly pooch to someone's bedside. Doing therapy dog work involves your own emotional stability as well as that of your dog. But once you have met all the requirements for this work, making the rounds once a week or once a month with your therapy dog is possibly the most rewarding of all community activities.

Disaster Aid

This community service is definitely not for everyone, partly because it is time-consuming. The initial training is rigorous, and there can be no let-up in the continuing workouts, because members are on call 24 hours a day to go wherever they are needed at a moment's notice. But if you think you would like to be able to assist in a disaster, look into search-and-rescue work. The network of search-and-rescue volunteers is worldwide, and all members of the American Rescue Dog Association (ARDA) who are qualified to do this work are volunteers who train and maintain their own dogs.

Physical Aid

Most people are familiar with Seeing Eye dogs, which serve as blind people's eyes, but not with all the other work that dogs are trained to do to assist the disabled. Dogs are also specially trained to pull wheelchairs, carry school books, pick up dropped objects, open and close doors. Some also are ears for the deaf. All these assistance-trained dogs, by the way, are allowed anywhere "No Pet" signs exist (as are therapy dogs when

Making the rounds with your therapy dog can be very rewarding.

properly identified). Getting started in any of this fascinating work requires a background in dog training and canine behavior, but there are also volunteer jobs ranging from answering the phone to cleaning out kennels to providing a foster home for a puppy. You have only to ask.

part four

Beyond
the
Basics

chapter 12

Recommended Reading

Books

ABOUT HEALTH CARE

Ackerman, Lowell. *Guide to Skin and Haircoat Problems in Dogs*. Loveland, Colo.: Alpine Publications, 1994.

Alderton, David. *The Dog Care Manual*. Hauppauge, N.Y.: Barron's Educational Series, Inc., 1986.

American Kennel Club. *American Kennel Club Dog Care and Training*. New York: Howell Book House, 1991.

Bamberger, Michelle, DVM. *Help! The Quick Guide to First Aid for Your Dog*. New York: Howell Book House, 1995.

Carlson, Delbert, DVM, and James Giffin, MD. *Dog Owner's Home Veterinary Handbook*. New York: Howell Book House, 1992.

DeBitetto, James, DVM, and Sarah Hodgson. *You & Your Puppy*. New York: Howell Book House, 1995.

Humphries, Jim, DVM. *Dr. Jim's Animal Clinic for Dogs*. New York: Howell Book House, 1994.

McGinnis, Terri. *The Well Dog Book*. New York: Random House, 1991.

Pitcairn, Richard and Susan. *Natural Health for Dogs*. Emmaus, Pa.: Rodale Press, 1982.

ABOUT DOG SHOWS

Hall, Lynn. *Dog Showing for Beginners*. New York: Howell Book House, 1994.

Nichols, Virginia Tuck. *How to Show Your Own Dog*. Neptune, N. J.: TFH, 1970.

Vanacore, Connie. *Dog Showing, An Owner's Guide*. New York: Howell Book House, 1990.

ABOUT TRAINING

Ammen, Amy. *Training in No Time*. New York: Howell Book House, 1995.

Baer, Ted. *Communicating With Your Dog*. Hauppauge, N.Y.: Barron's Educational Series, Inc., 1989.

Benjamin, Carol Lea. *Dog Problems*. New York: Howell Book House, 1989.

Benjamin, Carol Lea. *Dog Training for Kids*. New York: Howell Book House, 1988.

Benjamin, Carol Lea. *Mother Knows Best*. New York: Howell Book House, 1985.

Benjamin, Carol Lea. *Surviving Your Dog's Adolescence*. New York: Howell Book House, 1993.

Bohnenkamp, Gwen. *Manners for the Modern Dog*. San Francisco: Perfect Paws, 1990.

Dibra, Bashkim. *Dog Training by Bash*. New York: Dell, 1992.

Dunbar, Ian, PhD, MRCVS. *Dr. Dunbar's Good Little Dog Book*, James & Kenneth Publishers, 2140 Shattuck Ave. #2406, Berkeley, Calif. 94704. (510) 658–8588. Order from the publisher.

Dunbar, Ian, PhD, MRCVS. *How to Teach a New Dog Old Tricks*, James & Kenneth Publishers. Order from the publisher; address above.

Dunbar, Ian, PhD, MRCVS, and Gwen Bohnenkamp. Booklets on *Preventing Aggression; Housetraining; Chewing; Digging; Barking; Socialization; Fearfulness; and Fighting*, James & Kenneth Publishers. Order from the publisher; address above.

Evans, Job Michael. *People, Pooches and Problems*. New York: Howell Book House, 1991.

Kilcommons, Brian and Sarah Wilson. *Good Owners, Great Dogs*. New York: Warner Books, 1992.

McMains, Joel M. *Dog Logic—Companion Obedience*. New York: Howell Book House, 1992.

Rutherford, Clarice and David H. Neil, MRCVS. *How to Raise a Puppy You Can Live With*. Loveland, Colo.: Alpine Publications, 1982.

Volhard, Jack and Melissa Bartlett. *What All Good Dogs Should Know: The Sensible Way to Train*. New York: Howell Book House, 1991.

ABOUT BREEDING

Harris, Beth J. Finder. *Breeding a Litter, The Complete Book of Prenatal and Postnatal Care*. New York: Howell Book House, 1983.

Holst, Phyllis, DVM. *Canine Reproduction*. Loveland, Colo.: Alpine Publications, 1985.

Walkowicz, Chris and Bonnie Wilcox, DVM. *Successful Dog Breeding, The Complete Handbook of Canine Midwifery.* New York: Howell Book House, 1994.

ABOUT ACTIVITIES

American Rescue Dog Association. *Search and Rescue Dogs.* New York: Howell Book House, 1991.

Barwig, Susan and Stewart Hilliard. *Schutzhund.* New York: Howell Book House, 1991.

Beaman, Arthur S. *Lure Coursing.* New York: Howell Book House, 1994.

Daniels, Julie. *Enjoying Dog Agility—From Backyard to Competition.* New York: Doral Publishing, 1990.

Davis, Kathy Diamond. *Therapy Dogs.* New York: Howell Book House, 1992.

Gallup, Davis Anne. *Running With Man's Best Friend.* Loveland, Colo.: Alpine Publications, 1986.

Habgood, Dawn and Robert. *On the Road Again With Man's Best Friend.* New England, Mid-Atlantic, West Coast and Southeast editions. Selective guides to area bed and breakfasts, inns, hotels and resorts that welcome guests and their dogs. New York: Howell Book House, 1995.

Holland, Vergil S. *Herding Dogs.* New York: Howell Book House, 1994.

LaBelle, Charlene G. *Backpacking With Your Dog.* Loveland, Colo.: Alpine Publications, 1993.

Simmons-Moake, Jane. *Agility Training, The Fun Sport for All Dogs.* New York: Howell Book House, 1991.

Spencer, James B. *Hup! Training Flushing Spaniels the American Way.* New York: Howell Book House, 1992.

Spencer, James B. *Point! Training the All-Seasons Birddog.* New York: Howell Book House, 1995.

Tarrant, Bill. *Training the Hunting Retriever.* New York: Howell Book House, 1991.

Volhard, Jack and Wendy. *The Canine Good Citizen.* New York: Howell Book House, 1994.

General Titles

Haggerty, Captain Arthur J. *How to Get Your Pet Into Show Business.* New York: Howell Book House, 1994.

McLennan, Bardi. *Dogs and Kids, Parenting Tips.* New York: Howell Book House, 1993.

Moran, Patti J. *Pet Sitting for Profit, A Complete Manual for Professional Success.* New York: Howell Book House, 1992.

Scalisi, Danny and Libby Moses. *When Rover Just Won't Do, Over 2,000 Suggestions for Naming Your Dog.* New York: Howell Book House, 1993.

Sife, Wallace, PhD. *The Loss of a Pet.* New York: Howell Book House, 1993.

Wrede, Barbara J. *Civilizing Your Puppy.* Hauppauge, N.Y.: Barron's Educational Series, 1992.

Magazines

The AKC GAZETTE, The Official Journal for the Sport of Purebred Dogs. American Kennel Club, 51 Madison Ave., New York, NY.

Bloodlines Journal. United Kennel Club, 100 E. Kilgore Rd., Kalamazoo, MI.

Dog Fancy. Fancy Publications, 3 Burroughs, Irvine, CA 92718

Dog World. Maclean Hunter Publishing Corp., 29 N. Wacker Dr., Chicago, IL 60606.

Videos

"SIRIUS Puppy Training," by Ian Dunbar, PhD, MRCVS. James & Kenneth Publishers, 2140 Shattuck Ave. #2406, Berkeley, CA 94704. Order from the publisher.

"Training the Companion Dog," from Dr. Dunbar's British TV Series, James & Kenneth Publishers. (See address above).

The American Kennel Club produces videos on every breed of dog, as well as on hunting tests, field trials and other areas of interest to purebred dog owners. For more information, write to AKC/Video Fulfillment, 5580 Centerview Dr., Suite 200, Raleigh, NC 27606.

chapter 13

Resources

Breed Clubs

Every breed recognized by the American Kennel Club has a national (parent) club. National clubs are a great source of information on your breed. You can get the name of the secretary of the club by contacting:

The American Kennel Club
51 Madison Avenue
New York, NY 10010
(212) 696-8200

There are also numerous all-breed, individual breed, obedience, hunting and other special-interest dog clubs across the country. The American Kennel Club can provide you with a geographical list of clubs to find ones in your area. Contact them at the above address.

Registry Organizations

Registry organizations register purebred dogs. The American Kennel Club is the oldest and largest in this country, and currently recognizes over 130 breeds. The United Kennel Club registers some breeds the AKC doesn't (including the American Pit Bull Terrier and the Miniature Fox Terrier) as well as many of the same breeds. The others included here are for your reference; the AKC can provide you with a list of foreign registries.

American Kennel Club
51 Madison Avenue
New York, NY 10010

United Kennel Club (UKC)
100 E. Kilgore Road
Kalamazoo, MI 49001-5598

American Dog Breeders Assn.
P.O. Box 1771
Salt Lake City, UT 84110
(Registers American Pit Bull Terriers)

Canadian Kennel Club
89 Skyway Avenue
Etobicoke, Ontario
Canada M9W 6R4

National Stock Dog Registry
P.O. Box 402
Butler, IN 46721
(Registers working stock dogs)

Orthopedic Foundation for Animals (OFA)
2300 E. Nifong Blvd.
Columbia, MO 65201-3856
(Hip registry)

Activity Clubs

Write to these organizations for information on the activities they sponsor.

American Kennel Club
51 Madison Avenue
New York, NY 10010
(Conformation Shows, Obedience Trials, Field Trials and Hunting Tests, Agility, Canine Good

Citizen, Lure Coursing, Herding, Tracking,
Earthdog Tests, Coonhunting.)

United Kennel Club
100 E. Kilgore Road
Kalamazoo, MI 49001-5598
(Conformation Shows, Obedience Trials, Agility,
Hunting for Various Breeds, Terrier Trials and
more.)

North American Flyball Assn.
1342 Jeff St.
Ypsilanti, MI 48198

International Sled Dog Racing Assn.
P.O. Box 446
Norman, ID 83848-0446

North American Working Dog Assn., Inc.
Southeast Kreisgruppe
P.O. Box 833
Brunswick, GA 31521

Trainers

Association of Pet Dog Trainers
P.O. Box 3734
Salinas, CA 93912
(408) 663–9257

American Dog Trainers' Network
161 West 4th St.
New York, NY 10014
(212) 727–7257

**National Association of Dog Obedience
Instructors**
2286 East Steel Rd.
St. Johns, MI 48879

Associations

American Dog Owners Assn.
1654 Columbia Tpk.
Castleton, NY 12033
(Combats anti-dog legislation)

Delta Society
P.O. Box 1080
Renton, WA 98057-1080
(Promotes the human/animal bond through
pet-assisted therapy and other programs)

Dog Writers Assn. of America (DWAA)
Sally Cooper, Secy.
222 Woodchuck Ln.
Harwinton, CT 06791

National Assn. for Search and Rescue (NASAR)
P.O. Box 3709
Fairfax, VA 22038

Therapy Dogs International
1536 Morris Place
Hillside, NJ 07205